CANTERBURY

Text by
RICHARD MALTBY

Photographs by
ERNEST FRANKL

PEVENSEY
Heritage Guides

Canterbury

PLACES TO SEE

A Wholesale grocery and provisions warehouse, c.1880.

B Westgate House, c.1750.

C Falstaff Inn, 15th century but altered in 17th century.

D Westgate Grove, late 16th century.

E Tower House, c.1850, now the Mayor's Palace.

F Former Church of Holy Cross, 1374-81, since 1978 has served as the Guildhall.

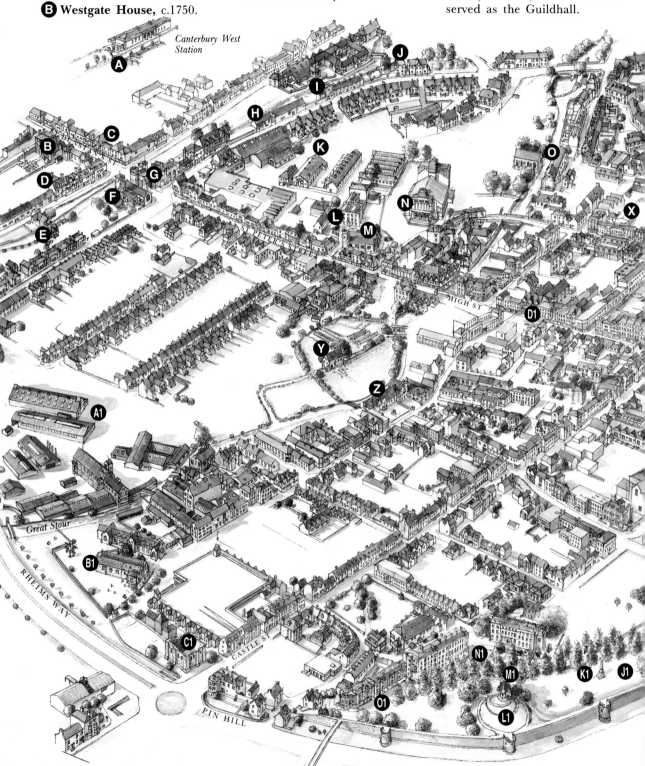

G Westgate, c.1380–mini fortress guarding the western entrance to the city.

H 16th-17th-century wool store built into remains of city wall.

I Sudbury Tower, c.1400.

L St Peter's House, c.1782.

M St Peter's Church, 13th century with remodelling. 14th-century tower.

N Marlowe Theatre, 1984, former Odeon cinema built 1933.

O Blackfriars, begun 1237 for Dominican Order. Now used by King's School as Arts Centre.

P Former synagogue, 1847. Front of Portland cement in Egyptian style.

V Site of Burgate, c.1475, demolished 1809.

W Canterbury Cathedral

X 15–12 Turn Again Lane, 15th century.

Y Remains of Greyfriars, c.1267.

Z Poor Priest's Hospital, c.1373. Since 1982 has served as Museum and Heritage Centre.

A1 St Mildred's Tannery

B1 Church of St Mildred, largely late 15th century.

C1 Castle, Norman keep, c.1109–25.

D1 Beaney Institute, Royal Museum and Free Library, 1897–9.

E1 Longmarket, reconstructed 1991–2.

F1 Roman Catholic Church of St Thomas à Becket, 1874–5, Gothic.

G1 St George's Church tower, 12–15th century. Church destroyed 1942.

H1 Site of former cattle market

I1 Don Jon Terrace, c.1800.

J1 Dane John Gardens, laid out 1790.

K1 South African War Memorial, 1904.

L1 Mound, c.1790, formed from motte of Norman Castle, of c.1070.

M1 Obelisk, 1803, in honour of Alderman James Simmons.

N1 Dane John Court, 1984.

O1 15–23 Don John Grove, 1822.

J 15th-century bastion of city wall.

K Westgate Hall, c.1920, originally territorial army drill hall.

Q St Radigund's Hall, 14th century.

R St Mary's Northgate, 13th century, rebuilt 1830, north wall built into medieval city wall.

S Green Court, first planted with lime trees in 1708.

T Memorial Garden

U Norman cemetery

Bus Station

A Pevensey Heritage Guide

Photographs: Ernest Frankl except front cover, 2: Skyscan Balloon Photography; 16 and back cover picture of Greyfriars: Richard Maltby

Colour map © Hubert Pragnell

A catalogue record for this book is available from the British Library.

ISBN 0 907115 64 0

Design by Book Production Consultants, Cambridge
Printed in Hong Kong by Wing King Tong Co. Ltd
for David & Charles plc
Brunel House Newton Abbot Devon

The Pevensey Press is an imprint of David & Charles plc

Front cover
Aerial view of Canterbury Cathedral and the city beyond (*Skyscan Balloon Photography*)

Back cover
The West Gate; Greyfriars, the oldest Franciscan building in Britain, viewed from Binnewith Meadow; Shops in the historic core of Canterbury, Burgate Street looking towards the Butter market

Title page inset (**1**)
The great West Window in the cathedral nave

Dedicated to Gwilym
The author's royalties will go to the Children's Liver Disease Foundation

Contents

THE APPROACHES TO CANTERBURY 7

A BRIEF HISTORY OF CANTERBURY 12

ST AUGUSTINE AND CANTERBURY 30

A PILGRIM'S PATH FROM THE EAST 32

A PILGRIM'S PATH FROM THE WEST 39

THE CATHEDRAL 51

THE PRECINCTS 69

GREEN COURT AND THE KING'S SCHOOL 82

THE DISTRICT OF CANTERBURY 92

Map of the city of Canterbury 2–3

The approaches to Canterbury

'The appearance of the City of Canterbury, from whatever part you approach it, is beautiful and equals the most sanguine expectation', wrote the Kent historian Edward Hasted, who saw Canterbury in the year 1800. 'The magnificent tower of the Cathedral strikes the eye as the principal object of admiration' and 'the surrounding hills encircling the whole, all together combine to form a prospect so pleasing, as is hardly to be exceeded anywhere for the extent of it.' Today the single most outstanding feature in almost every approach to Canterbury is still the Cathedral. To catch a glimpse of it signifies arrival at Canterbury.

The approaches by road are by some of the oldest routes in England. The road from Sandwich, which reaches Canterbury at St Martin's Hill, was the route from the Roman port of Rutupiae (Richborough). In AD 597, this was the way taken by St Augustine, who had stayed on the Isle of Thanet until King Ethelbert gave permission for him to come to Canterbury. In December 1170 this was also the route chosen by Archbishop Thomas Becket when he returned from France to his cathedral and eventual martyrdom. The windmill, one of only two tower mills in the county, is one of the best-known landmarks on the skyline of the city.

Until the 18th century the Old Dover Road was the main route taken by foreign visitors to the shrine of Becket, as a statute of 1385 obliged pilgrims to enter the country only at Dover. The New Dover Road, built in a straight line for a mile and a half from St George's Gate, was authorised by Act of Parliament in 1800. By then the Old Dover Road was too narrow and dangerous for stage-coaches and the new road helped stage-coaches to maintain an average speed of 9 mph between London and Dover.

The approaches by the Stour river valley offer occasional views of the Cathedral from a distance across meadows and open countryside. Upstream, a pre-Roman trackway running along the eastern bank of the Stour from Wye was the origin of the Thanington Road into Wincheap, a name derived from the Saxon Wenchiape, possibly a wine-market held outside the Wincheap gate. During the Middle Ages wool was brought from the southern downlands by this route for Canterbury's flourishing weaving industry. later the planting of extensive hop gardens added one of the best-known elements to the beauty of the Kentish countryside around. In 1724, Daniel Defoe noted, '... the ground round this city proves more particularly fruitful for the growth of hops than of any other production ... so that now they may say without boasting, there is at Canterbury the greatest plantation of hops in the whole island'. Downstream, the Sturry Road, which from Saxon times linked Canterbury with its port of Fordwich, has always been a busy route for merchandise and

2 Canterbury is the mother city of the Church of England, the seat of the archbishop and, for centuries, a place of pilgrimage. Today, over 2 million visitors come to Canterbury each year to make contact with the unique medieval city and the birthplace of Christianity in England

3 *Arriving from London, the visitor is suddenly confronted with this view of the Cathedral, just as it greeted pilgrims in centuries past*

heavy goods. In the Middle Ages, Caen stone used for building the Cathedral was imported at Fordwich and then taken on by road. Until the 18th century the Stour was navigable for barges and lighters and was used particularly for the transport of coal. Sturry Road leads to Military Road, a reminder that Canterbury has a long history as a garrison town.

The original Pilgrims' Way approached Canterbury from the direction of Harbledown and has been supplanted by the **Rheims Way** (**3**). Many pilgrims would have seen the fine views of the Cathedral that greet the visitor today. It was at Harbledown, just before entering the city, that one of Chaucer's pilgrims told the last of the *Canterbury Tales*:

> Woot ye nat where ther stant a litel toun,
> Which that ycleped is Bobbe-up-and-down
> Under the Blee, in Canterbury weye?

> Don't you all know where stands a little town,
> The one that people call Bob-up-and-down,
> Near Blean Woods on the way to Canterbury . . .

It was by this route that Henry II arrived at Canterbury in 1174 to do penance for Becket's murder. Another of many royal visitors was Elizabeth I, who courted and rejected marriage at Canterbury in 1573.

The high ridge to the north of the city, which runs between St Thomas' Hill and St Stephen's Hill and on which the University of Kent at Canterbury is

4 *The great West Gate: 'Two lofty turrets that command the town, I wonder how it could be conquered thus.' (Christopher Marlowe, The Jew of Malta)*

located, provides superb views of the Cathedral and the entire city. The best panoramic views are from vantage points in the University grounds and on its access road. The strong link between Canterbury and Whitstable makes St Thomas' Hill an important route, flanked by two more of the city's skyline landmarks, the Victorian buildings of St Edmund's School and the Water Tower. By this road Whitstable's oysters, much favoured by the Romans, were brought for consumption in Canterbury – trade developed as Whitstable replaced Fordwich as Canterbury's port. Blean Forest, through which routes from the north Kent coast to Canterbury pass, was for centuries notorious for highwaymen and smuggling bands, making the area a dangerous place for travel until the 19th century.

From the village of Tyler Hill, named after the pottery and tile industry that grew there in the 13th century, the road descends to the city at St Stephen's Hill, which again affords some very fine views. St Stephen's Green, encountered by forking left at the bottom of the hill, has retained its charming village character. It is bordered by **St Stephen's Church** (**5**) (the nave is 11th-century), 16th-century cottages and almshouses (Manwood's Hospital), the Victorian School House and the Olde Beverlie Inn.

The traveller by train from London or the coast arrives at either the East or West Station. Approaching the East Station on the line from London there are clear views of the Cathedral dominating the city. From the station a footbridge over the ring road leads directly on to the city wall and into the historic centre. Canterbury West, on the Ashford–Thanet line, is likely to be the point of arrival for visitors using the Channel Tunnel. The elegant station building was opened in 1846, but nearby an earlier line, the Canterbury and Whitstable Railway (known as the 'Crab and Winkle'), the world's first steam passenger railway, commenced service on 3 May 1830. Redevelopment of Canterbury West is planned, to provide a direct pedestrian link to the old city.

5 *St Stephen's Church, mostly 12th to 14th century and constructed of flint and stone, served the parish of Hackington where Archbishop Stephen Langton, around 1227, built a residence. For 300 years it was a favourite visiting place for archbishops*

A brief history of Canterbury

Canterbury is world famous as the centre of Christianity in England, and the Cathedral, founded by St Augustine in AD 597, is the mother church of the Anglican Communion throughout the world. Its archbishops are enthroned in St Augustine's Chair and since 1072, by the Accord of Winchester, the Archbishop of Canterbury has also been Primate of All England, giving his office at one time a power even over kings. The archbishopric is older than the kingship of a united England, twice as old as Parliament, twice as old as the ancient universities.

Canterbury also has a civic history of great distinction. It was a prosperous administrative and commercial centre under the Romans, and became the capital of the Saxon kingdom of Kent. Because of its geographical situation it has always been at the forefront of military and political events. 'Scarce any city of this realm is there to be preferred to this of ours in antiquity of origin or in dignity of fortune, or for that matter, to be compared with her,' declared John Twyne, Mayor of Canterbury, in the year 1540.

Roman Canterbury

The earliest settlement to have been revealed by archaeologists dates back to three hundred years before the time of Christ. It stood at the place where the trackways of the Kentish Downs converged to cross the River Stour, which to the north-east formed an estuary to the sea. When Julius Caesar came on his second expedition in 54 BC the Roman VIIth Legion stormed the Celtic hill-fort at Bigbury, just 3 miles west of the present city, but Caesar's expeditions were not followed up for a century. In the intervening period Canterbury became a permanent settlement and centre of trade with the name of Durwhern. When at the time of Emperor Claudius the Romans returned, in AD 43, the name they gave to the prosperous town that had developed here was Cantiacorum Durovernum: Durovernum after the Celtic name of Durwhern and Cantiacorum meaning of the Cantiaci or Kentish people.

The Roman city enjoyed the full benefits of the *Pax Romana*, having close trading links with the Continent by way of the three ports of Richborough (Rutupiae), Dover (Dubris) and Lympne (Lemanis). The roads from these ports converged on Canterbury to cross the Stour and then, as Watling Street, continued on for 55 miles to London. Canterbury was adorned with all the buildings expected in a major Roman city: a temple compound (measuring about 2 acres), public and private baths and a forum. The most outstanding building was the Roman amphitheatre, whose foundations may be seen in

6 A view from St Margaret's Street through Mercery Lane to the Christ Church Gate and the Cathedral beyond

cellars beneath **St Margaret's Street** (**6**). It was probably the largest amphitheatre north of the Alps. This enormous D-shaped building had a diameter of 232 feet, stood about 60 feet high, had an outer wall more than 6 feet thick and would have seated three thousand people. The foundations of the Roman city wall, built between AD 270 and 290, lie beneath the existing walls. A large section of it, with crenellations, is incorporated into St Mary's Church in Northgate, and Roman archway can be seen embedded in the medieval wall at Queningate.

One of the most exciting finds ever to be discovered in Canterbury was a hoard of silver, buried about AD 410, which included some silver spoons bearing the Greek letters chi rho, the first two letters of Christ's name. The chi rho monogram shows that Christianity was well established at Canterbury towards the end of the Roman era. The silver is displayed in the 'Time Walk' Heritage Museum. In Butchery Lane a large portion of a Roman town house has been uncovered with an extensive mosaic floor, and as excavations of the Longmarket continue there are likely to be many more Roman finds.

The Saxon Centuries

After the Romans left Britain, the country was overrun by Anglo-Saxon tribes from the near Continent. The Roman city fell into decay and the grid street pattern was irrevocably lost, but there are traces of continuing city life through the Dark Ages. In 1981 an excavation unearthed a 5th-century family burial of parents, two daughters and even the household dogs. The family was buried with ceremony and was adorned with a mixture of late Roman and Saxon jewellery. The discovery suggests that at Canterbury Roman and Saxon cultures coexisted without the destruction experienced in most parts of the country.

When in 560 King Ethelbert of Kent married the Christian Frankish Princess Bertha, Saxon Canterbury or Cantwarabyrig – meaning Kentish people's Stronghold – was trading in fine jewellery with the Continent and was the goal of St Augustine's mission from Pope Gregory to the English people. The story is told in *The Ecclesiastical History of the English People*, written by the Venerable Bede in 731. Ethelbert met Augustine in Thanet, according to Bede in the open air because the King was fearful of the 'magical arts' the missionary might use upon him. 'But', Bede continues, 'the monks were endowed with power from God, not the Devil, and approached the King carrying a silver cross as their standard and the likeness of Our Lord and Saviour painted on a Cross.' Augustine was allowed to preach, and to use **St Martin's Church** (**7**), a church founded in Roman times which had served as a chapel for Queen Bertha. It was probably here on Whitsunday 597 that Ethelbert was baptised. The association of St Augustine and King Ethelbert, the latter acknowledged as 'Bretwalda' (Britain Ruler) and also author of the first written code of English Law, was the basis of Canterbury's future greatness. With the King's support Augustine first established a monastery, the Abbey of St Peter and St Paul, which was later to be known as the Abbey of St. Augustine. Some ruins of the Abbey remain; it was located outside the city wall in accordance with the Roman custom of not permitting burials within the confines of a town. Here were the mausolea of Augustine, Ethelbert and succeeding kings and archbishops through the Saxon centuries. In 602

7 *St Martin's Church: a view of the south sides of the nave and chancel, showing extensive sections of Roman and Saxon walling*

OVERLEAF

8 *The Dane John Mound was shaped to its present height by Alderman James Simmons in the works undertaken in the gardens between 1790 and 1804. Circular pathways lead up to the stone monument at the summit, from which there are five views across the city*

Augustine also established Christ Church, on the site of an earlier church, as his cathedral. The little Saxon church of St Mildred's, named after the great-great-granddaughter of Ethelbert, shows that Christianity became a strong force in the city.

By the early 8th century Canterbury was clearly established as the focus of English Christianity. Under the inspiration of Archbishop Theordore (669–92) and his close associate, Abbot Hadrian, the fame of the monastic school had spread from Northumbria to Rome. After the centre of government transferred to Wessex in the mid-9th century, kings still conferred privileges on the city and endowed its monastic houses with more land. Mints existed here in the Saxon period and coins dating from the early 8th century have been found.

Kent suffered severely over the following two hundred years from Viking raids. Canterbury was pillaged in 851 and again, despite paying tribute to the Vikings, in 865. The disasters culminated in the sack of the city and Cathedral in 1011, when Archbishop Alphege was taken captive. Having forbidden the payment of any ransom, the Archbishop was later horribly murdered by the Vikings. According to the Anglo-Saxon Chronicle, in the course of a drunken brawl they 'pelted him to death with bones and the heads of cattle'.

The Middle Ages

9 *One of the original royal castles of Kent (the other two are at Rochester and Dover), Canterbury Castle was built soon after the Battle of Hastings. The stone keep pictured dates from the reign of Henry I. For centuries the Castle's main use was as a prison for the County of Kent. It fell into ruin in the 18th century, but the remains are now conserved as a national monument*

The medieval buildings we see in Canterbury today are largely the legacy of two great bursts of building activity, after the Norman Conquest (1066) and after the Black Death (1348). The first archbishop after the Conquest was Lanfranc, and it was he who rebuilt the Cathedral (it had been destroyed by a fire just before the Conquest), established Christ Church Priory, which became the largest monastery in England, and founded St John's Hospital and St Gregory's Priory. After the Conquest, St Augustine's Abbey was also entirely rebuilt and greatly enlarged. **Dane John** (**8**) (from the Norman 'donjon'), originally a burial mound, was part of an enormous motte-and-bailey castle. Further fortification was provided by the **Norman stone keep** (**9**) (the original structure was a storey higher than the surviving remains) and the Norman wall. This followed the **Roman wall** (**10**), and had 21 towers

17

and 8 gateways, of which the **West Gate** (**4**) is the sole, magnificent survivor. In addition, two parish churches, 8 street markets, 7 watermills, 30 stone-cellared merchant houses and a guildhall were established. To fit in the Archbishop's Palace, Lanfranc pushed out the line of the street, as can be seen where it kinks past the Mint Yard into Palace Street.

Canterbury's growth was all the more favoured by its geographical position between London and Dover when kings of England also ruled half of France. The most famous event in Canterbury's history, the murder of Archbishop Thomas Becket, was to make it even more important. Thomas Becket, a man of humble origins, rose to become Chancellor and constant companion of King Henry II (1154–89). In 1161, on the death of Archbishop Theobald, Henry had Becket elected Archbishop, hoping to secure in him an ally in

10 The medieval walls built on earlier Roman foundations define the limits of the old city

11 The Blackfriars. Of the Dominican friary, once the hub of this part of Canterbury, only two parts survive: the refectory (pictured) and the guest hall, which face each other across this delightful riverside scene

building a strong monarchical state. Becket, however, immediately resigned the chancellorship, rejected his old way of life and insisted, against the King's will, on preserving the rights and independence of the Church. After a dramatic confrontation, Becket went into exile in France and excommunicated his enemies. Henry retaliated by confiscating church revenues and having Becket's relatives and friends banished or thrown into prison.

By the end of 1170, perhaps realising that it would take nothing less than his martyrdom to save his cause, Becket returned to Canterbury and on Christmas Day delivered a sermon that would provoke the King. Henry responded with his famous cry. 'Who will rid me of this turbulent priest?' Four knights, Richard Brito, Hugh de Moreville, Reginald FitzUrse and William de Tracy, hurried across the Channel and, thinking they had understood Henry's meaning, pursued Becket from the Archbishop's Palace into the Cathedral, where they slaughtered him. According to a monastic chronicle, the fatal blow severed the crown of Becket's head, 'in such a way that the blood white with the brain and the brain no less red with the blood, dyed the floor of the Cathedral with the white of the lily and the red of the rose'.

The martyrdom of Becket, Henry II's spectacular penance in 1174 and St Thomas' canonisation put Canterbury in a class of pilgrim centre with Rome and Compostella in the medieval Christian world. Just six weeks after Henry came to do his penance a fire destroyed most of the Norman choir. Work began at once on the reconstruction of the east end of the Cathedral. The result was one of the finest Cathedral buildings in the Gothic or Early English style. Canterbury became a pilgrim city, especially after 1220 when King Henry III headed the procession in which the saint's body was transferred from the crypt to its jewelled shrine in Trinity Chapel. For three and a half centuries the shrine of St Thomas Becket attracted thousands of pilgrims not only from England but from all over Europe. It was at its most popular in the later part of the 14th century, at about the time Geoffrey Chaucer was writing the *Canterbury Tales*.

Accommodation for the pilgrims was continually expanded. Within the Priory, Chillenden's Chambers and Meister Omers were built on a spacious scale. St Augustine's, eclipsed as a shrine by Becket's martyrdom, also offered guest halls. Both inside and outside the city many inns were founded or enlarged. The Chequers of Hope once occupied the whole western side of Mercery Lane. Liberty's store in Burgate Street was originally a guest house and, outside the Westgate, the Falstaff was built especially to accommodate pilgrims who arrived to find the city gates closed for the night. One of the best preserved of these halls is the restored hospital for poor priests founded in the early 13th century near the river in Stour Street. It now houses the 'Time Walk' Heritage Museum of the city's history.

The religious foundations of the city were completed by the arrival and settlement of the friars. The Dominicans, known as Blackfriars on account of the black coat they wore over their white habits, first came to the city in 1221. In 1237 they were granted land by Henry III on an island in the Stour where the **Blackfriars Refectory** (**11**) and Guesthouse still stand alongside the banks of the river. The first group of Franciscans, followers of St Francis of Assisi, landed at Dover and made their way to Canterbury in 1224. They were the Greyfriars, dressed in ragged, grey habits and walking barefoot. They

12 *Poor Priests' Hospital was founded in 1220 as a hospital 'for the poor and indigent priests' and soon afterwards was used to house the first Grey Friars to come to England. The Poor Priests' in more recent centuries has been used as a gaol and a workhouse. It now houses the city's 'Time-Walk' Heritage Museum*

were welcomed by the monks of Christ Church and housed in the **Poor Priests' Hospital** (**12**), until in 1267 they were given the marshy and flood-prone area known as the Island of Binnewith. Today only part of their building survives but, standing on two pointed arches over the river, it is one of the most picturesque medieval remains in Canterbury. The Franciscans tended the many sick and poor of this part of the city and also poor, infirm pilgrims at St Thomas' Hospital on the Eastbridge. The Whitefriars or Austin Friars arrived in the 14th century at the site now covered by the Whitefriars shopping precinct.

The Age of Chaucer was synonymous with the Age of Chivalry and, for the English during the Hundred Years War, the Black Prince (1330–76), whose tomb is in the Cathedral, epitomised the chivalric values of Chaucer's 'very perfect, gentle knight'. The *Canterbury Tales* remind us that it was also an age of a flowering vernacular literature, when English was established as the national language. At the turn of the 14th and 15th centuries Gothic architecture reached glorious heights in the Perpendicular nave of the Cathedral, completed in 1405 by the greatest builder of the time, Henry Yevele. From this period also date the great Bell Harry Tower, begun in 1494, and the Great Cloister (1397–1414), in which the painted bosses of the lierne vaulting comprise the largest collection of heraldry in England.

Chaucer (c. 1342–1400) also lived through some dreadful events, such as the recurrence of the deadly bubonic plague following the Black Death (1348). Half the population of Canterbury was wiped out. The Cathedral monks were not spared and three Masters of the Eastbridge Hospital died of the plague. Their revenue hit, the monasteries intensified labour services while surviving peasants wanted freedom. These tensions boiled over in the Peasants' Revolt (1381), when insurrectionary peasants ransacked the Cathedral and Archbishop's Palace, before storming the Castle, setting free the prisoners, and marching to London. Archbishop Sudbury, who as Chancellor was held responsible for the hated poll tax, fled to London, only to be seized there and hacked to death. Completed in the very same year as the Peasants' Revolt, 1381, the Westgate Towers are massive symbols of the turmoil of the Chaucerian age.

13 *St Dunstan's Church, originally a late-Saxon or early-Norman church and largely rebuilt in the Middle Ages. It was here, in 1174, that Henry II stripped off his clothes and put on the hair shirt and woollen dress of a penitential pilgrim before walking barefoot through the streets to the Cathedral*

From the Dissolution of the Monasteries to the Civil War

Canterbury's greatest challenge came when, following his breach with Rome in 1534, Henry VIII dissolved the monasteries and destroyed the shrine of Becket. St Augustine's Abbey was largely demolished, although the Abbbot's Lodgings were preserved and adapted as the King's House for the use of royal visitors. The Priory of Christ was dissolved in 1539 and replaced by a new foundation of a dean and 12 prebends. By the same statutes, the monastic school was refounded in 1541 as the King's School, with an endowment of 50 poor scholars. One of the school's best-known pupils was the Canterbury-born Elizabethan poet and playwright, Christopher Marlowe (1564–93), whose plays include *Edward II, Tamburlaine* and *Doctor Faustus*. A charming memorial in the Dane John Gardens and the Marlowe Theatre commemorate the city's most famous literary figure.

In Canterbury the first Catholic martyr was Father John Stone, a Whitefriar, who was boiled in oil, hanged and dismembered at the Dane John field. St Thomas More, executed in 1535, is also remembered at Canterbury. His head was brought here by his daughter Margaret and placed in the vault beneath **St Dunstan's Church** (**13**). The first martyrs for the Protestant faith, in Mary's reign (1553–58), were mainly ordinary folk from the villages around. Some died of starvation in the Castle, but altogether 30 men and 11 women were burned at the stake. A stone memorial stands in Martyrs' Field Road surmounted by a Canterbury Cross with its rounded arms, the characteristic symbol of the city.

During the reign of Elizabeth I (1558–1601) the city welcomed a large number of religious refugees from the Continent. The Huguenots from the Low Countries and France brought their weaving skills with them. Immigration accelerated after the Massacre of St Bartholomew at Paris in 1572, and the number of foreign weavers in Canterbury rose to 1,300 in 126 establishments employing another 2,500 workers. They settled in riverside parishes where water power was freely available; their splendid timber-framed houses can be seen in many parts of the city. Elizabeth I granted the Huguenots the use of the Black Prince's Chantry in the Cathedral crypt for their worship, and a French Protestant service is still regularly held there.

When in the early 1600s local Puritans were hounded by the authorities, Robert Cushman, a grocer's assistant, was forced to leave Canterbury and seek refuge in Holland. He returned 12 years later and negotiated from an inn in Palace Street the hire of the *Mayflower*, the ship which was to take the Pilgrim Fathers to Cape Cod in 1620. A number of Canterbury families sailed with the Cushmans to start a new life in America.

The Cathedral suffered greatly as a consequence of the Civil War. In 1643 Colonel Sandys and 41 musketeers were sent from London to secure the city for Parliament. The soldiers attacked everything they considered 'popish', especially a statue of Christ which stood above the Christ Church Gate. Worse damage followed when Canterbury's Puritan Mayor, supported by a fanatical clergyman known as Blue Dick, systematically smashed stained-glass windows and statues of saints within the Cathedral. By December 1647 the citizens of Canterbury had suffered enough of Puritan rule. A Parliamentary decree ordering that there should be no celebration of Christmas Day was the last straw. The Mayor was mobbed and thrown into a gutter,

and Royalists seized control. With only 1,300 men to defend it, however, Canterbury was no match for the advancing New Model Army under the command of General Ireton. On Cromwell's orders the city gates were pulled from their hinges and burnt, a 50-yard section of the city wall was breached and levelled near **St Mildred's** (**14**), and the Archbishop's Palace, second in size only to Westminster Hall, was destroyed. In 1660 Charles II spent the first night of his return from exile in Canterbury. He was so shocked by the damage to the Cathedral interior that he immediately donated money for new choir stalls.

The 18th and 19th centuries

The Restoration ushered in a long period of peace and stability. The development of hop farming in the countryside around Canterbury brought a new source of prosperity, while the coaching industry provided two thousand jobs. In the heyday of coaching, four daily departures reached London in six hours by stage-coaches such as the *Tallyho, Express* and *Phoenix*. The traveller had the choice of eight hotels and 69 taverns. Livery stables, coach-builders and blacksmiths flourished.

Alderman James Simmons (1741–1807) was an outstanding example of local enterprise. Twice Mayor and Member of Parliament for the city, he founded the Canterbury Bank and owned the *Kentish Gazette*. He largely financed the laying out of the fine tree-lined avenues of the Dane John

14 St Mildred's Church, the oldest church within the city walls, reveals substantial 8th-century work in the south and west wall, including massive stone corner quoins. St Mildred, great-great granddaughter of King Ethelbert, was a popular local saint. Izaak Walton, author of The Compleat Angler, *was married here in 1626, appropriately, since the river flows nearby*

Gardens and the landscaping of the old motte-and-bailey mound. In the years of Alderman Simmons, Canterbury acquired all the amenities of a county capital: an Assembly Rooms, Theatre, Philosophical Institute, Hospital – named the Kent and Canterbury and established in 1791 – and a Sessions House with a 'County Gaol and House of Correction'. The elegant houses of the Dane John Gardens and St Dunstan's are the most obvious legacy of the Georgian era. Contemporary directories list 349 'Nobles, Clergy, Gentry and Retired Persons' as giving 'tone and trade' to the city, together with 21 solicitors, 22 medical men, 12 surveyors and 27 corn dealers among the middle classes. The great Prime Minister Pitt the Younger and the Prince Regent accepted the honour of the Freedom of the City. Another visitor was Emma Hamilton, following the death of Lord Nelson at the Battle of Trafalgar (1805); she often came to the Cathedral Precincts, in which Nelson's brother was a canon from 1803 to 1838. More trade was brought to the city with the establishment of a garrison of 2,500 soldiers beyond Northgate following the outbreak of war with revolutionary France in 1793. The military museum of the Buffs, linked with Canterbury since 1573 and one of the country's oldest regiments, commemorates its long and distinguished history.

Unfortunately many of the 'improvements' brought about by the Commission established in 1769 for 'Paving, Lighting and Watching the Streets' destroyed much of the medieval fabric of the city. To widen the streets all the gateways except the Westgate were demolished. Projections from houses were cut back to a maximum 12 inches, as can be seen in St Peter's Street, where many timber houses were refaced with false bricks. A real improvement was carried out to the King's Bridge, which was widened and improved.

3 May 1830 saw the opening of the Canterbury and Whitstable Railway. Built by the Stephensons, the railway was only 6½ miles long, but its notable firsts are not widely known. Canterbury had the first ever steam hauled passenger service (three months before the better known Liverpool and Manchester Railway), the first railway tunnel (under Tyler Hill), the first season tickets and the first combined rail-steam ship fares with direct connections for London. The railway brought the benefit of cheap coal, but the line was eventually closed in 1953. Parts of the track way can still be walked and a plaque commemorates the line at the charming West Station. The original locomotive, the 'Invicta', is housed in the Heritage Museum.

Kent is one of the counties where the game of cricket began. The Kent County Cricket Club has its origins at St Stephen's in the Olde Beverlie Inn, where an ancient bat-and-ball game is still played in the garden. In 1847 the club moved to the St Lawrence Cricket Ground, famous for the tree within the field of play. In early August, Canterbury's cricket week is one of the highlights of the city's social calendar.

In the 19th century Canterbury attracted the interest of artists and writers, including J.M.W. Turner, who painted a dozen pictures here, most notable *St Anselm's Chapel and the Corona at the Cathedral*. Canterbury was a favourite haunt of Charles Dickens and features prominently in his *David Copperfield*. The animal painter and Royal Academician Sidney Cooper was born here, as was Mary Tourtel, creator of the children's classic character Rupert Bear (she lived in Palace Street); and it was here that the sea-loving novelist Joseph Conrad died, having spent the last years of his life at nearby Bishopsbourne.

World War II and after

During its long and eventful history Canterbury has experienced and survived many crises. Death and destruction came during once more in the night of 1 June 1942, when high explosive and incendiary bombs rained down on the city. There was massive destruction in the St George's area, the Cathedral Library received a direct hit and bombs fell on other parts of the Precincts. Miraculously the Cathedral survived. The visitor can see how complete the ruin was by realising that the only historic building in the High Street east of Longmarket is **St George's Tower (15)**.

After the war fierce controversy raged over plans for the redevelopment of the city centre. Victory for the 'anti-planners' in municipal elections meant that no coherent scheme was carried through. The structures built in the 1950s and 1960s are at best mediocre and at worst a disgrace; although a brighter note was the thoroughly appropriate decision to locate here the University of Kent at Canterbury, which opened its doors in 1965. Fortunately, since local government reorganisation in 1974, greater sensitivity has been shown towards conservation, one excellent result being the pedestrianisation of the historic centre of the city.

Canterbury Today And Tomorrow

Canterbury's character is a product of the intermeshing of historic, religious and educational factors and its compact size in a valley setting. The city centre is still largely defined by the medieval city walls, the Cathedral remains the dominant element, as it has been for centuries, and the city is still surrounded by large areas of open fields, parkland and woodland which provide both a visual backdrop and vantage points for panoramic views. The old city is predominantly composed of medieval timber-framed buildings, albeit often with an 18th-century veneer, with steeply pitched tile roofs. It is also a city where people have lived and worked for over two thousand years, and where distinct communities have carried on their daily lives. It is an image, however, that in the late 20th century has become harder to preserve, given the ever-increasing commercial and tourist pressures that Canterbury increasingly attracts. St Peter's, until the 1980s, was a self-contained village community within the city walls; St Dunstan's, beyond the Westgate Towers, just about hangs on.

Tourism, for centuries a major source of Canterbury's livelihood, now brings two million visitors to the Cathedral each year. Organised school and educational visits come not only from London, but from far beyond, including the near Continent. With the opening of the Channel Tunnel in 1993, Canterbury is even more accessible for foreign visitors. Visitors are becoming increasingly sophisticated, expecting higher standards of provision and preservation of the city's heritage. The problem is how to accommodate thousands of visitors all the year round without destroying the place they have come to see. Canterbury has also developed as a prosperous commercial centre. The future of the city will depend on retaining its character and ethos, and managing the pressures of commerce and tourism without stultifying development and growth. This is, however, a far from easy equation to solve in a relatively small city. City Council attempts during the 1980s to provide amenities for visitors foundered because they would have spoilt the environment which the visitors (and residents) wish to enjoy.

The redevelopment of bombed sites in the city centre in the aftermath of World War II, with large modern buildings in unsympathetic materials and completely out of proportion with the character of the historic city, is now widely condemned as a planning disaster. To avoid any repetition and to enhance the existing historic buildings in the city centre, a Conservation Area was established in the 1970s within which all building is subject to strict control. Some of the very poor developments of the 1950s, particularly in the Longmarket and St George's Tower area, have already been or will soon be demolished and rebuilt. Canterbury has taken its second chance in the 20th century to rebuild the commercial centre.

The new **Longmarket** development was especially contentious because it concerned the very centre of the old city in the shadow of the Bell Harry Tower. When a City Council scheme in 1987 proposed to replace the ugly 1950s buildings with new shops and offices with medieval-looking façades in imitation of the original buildings destroyed in the war, it was criticised as the worst case of film-set architecture to be proposed in Canterbury; but the outcome, with its provision for an underground Roman Museum, is more successful than was at first feared. An attractive plaza area meets a need for

public space, while the frontage along **Butchery Lane** (**16**) has restored the character and sense of enclosure of this historic street. It now frames one of the most delightful views of the Bell Harry Tower.

This is not to deny the success of some of the schemes of the 1980s, such as the attractive Regency development in Castle Way, for instance. Certainly the rebuilding of damaged or partly destroyed medieval buildings, the Templars in St Dunstan's for example, is to be encouraged. Within the Cathedral Precincts, Luxmoore House, built in 1981 as an addition to the King's School by Maguire and Murray, is commended by Prince Charles in his book *A Vision of Britain* for its qualities of sensitivity and care.

Commerce has combined with conservation so that many of Canterbury's historic buildings have been restored by local businesses and opened to the public. Not to be missed is Conquest House in Palace Street, a building of outstanding interest with an 11th-century stone cellar, reputedly where the four knights armed themselves before seeking out Thomas Becket, and a splendid, timber-framed 13th-century gallery. Beautifully restored and now open as an antiques store, the interior of Conquest House is an architectural delight. Much the same can be said of Liberty's in the Burgate, Cogan House in St Peter's Street, and, most recently, Crump's in Best Lane, where the room in the roof space of this superbly restored medieval hall is used as an art gallery. These are just some of the notable successes where local enterprise has embraced conservation to show how the pressures on the historic fabric of Canterbury can be channelled and resolved.

Commercial sponsorship has also underpinned the annual Chaucer Festival in April and the Canterbury Festival in October – the latter consisting of three weeks of concerts, opera, drama, dance, excursions and talks – which have become highlights of Canterbury life.

St Augustine and Canterbury

The coming of St Augustine to Canterbury is one of the most famous events in English history. Augustine was Abbot of the monastery of St Andrew in Rome and was sent in AD 597 by Pope Gregory the Great to convert England to Christianity. (A Bible believed to have been given by Pope Gregory to St Augustine is in the library of Corpus Christi College, Cambridge, and is used in our own time in the accession ceremony of the Archbishops of Canterbury.) Augustine arrived in Canterbury with 40 companions from the Isle of Thanet, King Ethelbert having granted him freedom to preach and a dwelling place in the city. 'Tradition says', according to Bede, 'that as they approached the

17 *St Martin's Font. Bede relates: 'When he [King Ethelbert], among the rest, induced by the unspotted life of these holy men and their delightful promises, which, by many miracles, they proved to be most certain, believed and was baptised, greater numbers began daily to flock together to hear the word, and forsaking their heathen rites, to associate themselves, by believing, to the unity of the Church of Christ.' Experts now think the 'Saxon Font' to be largely a medieval replica*

city, bearing the holy cross and the likeness of our great King and Lord Jesus Christ as was their custom, they sang in unison this litany: "We pray Thee, O Lord, in all Thy mercy, that Thy wrath and anger may be turned away from this city and from Thy holy house, for we are sinners. Alleluia."' In all probability the party came along the old Roman road from the direction of Richborough over the top of the hill to set up their headquarters at **St Martin's Church**.

St Martin's is probably the oldest identifiable Christian site in England. St Martin of Tours, after whom the church is named, died in AD 395 having lived to a great age, and many think the church was founded or rededicated in his lifetime. Extensive areas of Roman brickwork are still visible in the church walls, and Bede dates the foundation of St Martin's back to the early Christians, when the Romans still occupied the country. He says, 'On the east side of the city stood an old church, built in honour of Saint Martin during the Roman occupation of Britain, where the Christian queen of whom I have spoken went to pray.' The queen was Bertha, the Christian daughter of the King of Paris, who married Ethelbert. Their marriage treaty gave her freedom to practise her faith. The general opinion is that Queen Bertha used this building or one on its site for her devotions, but we cannot be certain whether she found a Christian building already there, or whether she converted a heathen temple, turning the ancient site into a Christian church under the guidance of her chaplain, Liudhard.

From Bede's simple statement we can conjure up a picture of the Queen making her way each day to the little church on the hillside, where she prayed for the conversion of her husband and his people. Her vigil lasted 35 years. it was crowned with success with the coming of Augustine and, soon after, the adoption of the Christian faith by King Ethelbert. He was baptised by Augustine, probably in St Martin's. One of the most beautiful features in the church is the decorated font (**17**), and some suppose that it served for the baptism of King Ethelbert although its date is disputed.

A Pilgrim's path from the East

For 350 years Canterbury was one of the Christian world's chief places of pilgrimage, perhaps surpassed only by Jerusalem and Rome. 'This Citie hath been chiefly maintained by two things', wrote the Protestant Lambarde. 'First, by the residence and Hospitalitie of the Archbishop and Religious persons, and then by the liberalitie and expense of such as either gadded to St Thomas for help and devotion, or travelled towards the sea side for their private affairs and business.' The comment could well apply to modern tourism.

The first stop on the outskirts of Canterbury for pilgrims coming from the Continent to the shrine of St Thomas would have been St Martin's. In the garden across the lane from the lychgate the spring of water is the first indication of why people in ancient times regarded this site as a holy place. The 14th-century flint tower of the church just manages to rise above the trees. In the graveyard, headstones, tombs, trees and shrubs complete the setting. From the path around the little church there is a fine view of the great Cathedral beyond.

Inside St Martin's some Roman brickwork is exposed on the chancel walls. The original Roman doorway, with stone blocks forming the lintel and sill, can be best seen from outside; the rounded **Saxon doorway** (**18**) was inserted at a later date. It is thought that originally what is today the west half of the chancel was the chapel used by Queen Bertha and her chaplain, as the rest of the Roman building was in ruins. The church was subsequently enlarged by restoring the original Roman building as the nave. Today the stonework of the west wall is completely exposed, revealing the rather irregular re-use of red Roman tiles. It is likely that the rebuilding was carried out under Augustine's directions as Bede records. 'Here [at St Martin's] they first assembled to sing the psalms, to pray, to say Mass and to baptise.' In the same sentence Bede adds that King Ethelbert gave Augustine permission to build and repair churches everywhere.

The church's story is told in the stained glass windows, fragments of which date from the 15th century. There are scenes from the life and death of St Martin and the death of the Venerable Bede. In the Victorian window above the altar the story of St Augustine is retold: Bertha and her maidens at worship at St Martin's; Augustine landing at Ebbsfleet on the Isle of Thanet; Augustine proceeding into Canterbury with his companions; and the baptism of Ethelbert by Augustine.

From the church the road to the city leads down Longport, the final section

18 *The Saxon doorway piercing the wall was an addition to the tiny chancel of St Martin's Church. The wall itself is built of Roman tiles. This part of the church probably formed the chapel of Queen Bertha*

of the Pilgrims' Way from Dover to Canterbury. Near St Martin's are the single-storey, timber-framed Smith's Almshouses, built in 1657 and dated in great metal numbers on the gable. On the right are the prison and the St Augustine's Session House by the architect George Byfield (1808), with a notable iron fence decorated with the fasces, symbol of authority. The Kent and Canterbury Hospital was first built between 1791 and 1793 on part of the former Abbey precinct and the site now forms an attractive public garden. The name of the Longport, at the coach park, is derived from its use as a long, open street market.

St Augustine's Abbey

After Ethelbert's baptism Augustine went back to France and was consecrated Bishop of 'the English Nation'. He returned to establish his episcopal see in Canterbury and proceeded with Ethelbert's help to build a cathedral church, the predecessor of the present Cathedral. Outside the city walls Augustine founded a monastery as a burial place for the kings of Kent and for himself and his successors as archbishops of Canterbury. The Abbey of St Peter and St Paul was founded in 598, later to be rededicated as St Augustine's.

St Augustine's Abbey (**19**) was largely destroyed in 1538 at the Dissolution of the Monasteries, but is still a marvellous place to walk about in, and its remains have been brought fully to light by excavations. The original Saxon monastery was a line of churches running directly east–west. To the west was a chapel and to the east, in succession, the Abbey Church of SS Peter and Paul, the Church of St Mary and the Chapel of St Pancras. The Abbey Church had side chapels and here were buried the most important people, archbishops in St Gregory's Chapel to the north and kings in St Martin's Chapel to the south. Augustine himself was buried to the south of the altar in St Gregory's Chapel. A small portion of the chapel has survived among the

19 St Augustine's: the remains of the 11th-century great nave of the abbey church were incorporated in the King's House built for Henry VIII. Tudor brickwork stands out above the Norman arches

20 The arch of the early 7th-century Chapel of St Pancras, with plainly visible Roman bricks

ruins and a shelter covers the site of the empty tombs of Archbishops Lawrence, Justus and Mellitus.

The remains of the easternmost church, **St Pancras (20)**, have survived well and parts stand almost to their full height. It was long thought that this building served as King Ethelbert's idol house before his conversion to Christianity and was changed to a church by Augustine. The Roman brick and columns of which the walls are partly made were here even before the Saxons came, but the structure provides abundant evidence that it belongs to the time of Augustine.

By the early 8th century the Abbey was famous for its schools and beautiful illuminated manuscripts. Despite the Viking raids, monastic life continued and took on fresh inspiration when the Abbey Church was enlarged by St Dunstan and rededicated to St Augustine in 978. In the 1050s Abbot Wulfric II began to construct an octagonal rotunda to link the Abbey Church and St Mary's together. The work was never completed, but the lowest part of Wulfric's rotunda survives and is unique in this country.

After the Norman Conquest St Augustine's was entirely rebuilt by Abbot Scotland (1070–87) and his successor Abbot Wido (1087–99). The bodies of Augustine and the other early archbishops were transferred to new tombs in the reconstructed Abbey, which must have contained the most impressive collection of shrines in England. A great part of the crypt still remains. The vault of the eastern chapel (Our Lady of the Angels) has been restored and the chapel is occasionally used. A section of the north wall of the nave also stands, where six stone arches survived to form the south side of the wall of Henry VIII's King's House. The mass to the left of the wall is the base of Ethelbert's tower, which stood until 1822.

Some important buildings survived the dissolution of the Abbey, which occurred in the last three months of 1539. The lodgings of the abbot of St Augustine's were spared, not for religious reasons, but because they were converted to serve as the King's Lodging House. Elizabeth I stayed here when she celebrated for fortieth birthday at Canterbury in 1573, and in 1625 the Gateway Chamber served as the bridal suite for Charles I and Henrietta Maria.

By that time the Abbey Precincts had been covered with soil and planted as an elaborate garden with fountains and mazes. It was here that the famous botanists John Tradescant (c. 1570–1638) and his son John (1608–62) were responsible for cultivating many plants previously unknown in this country. In 1618 the elder Tradescant travelled to Russia and two years later he joined an expedition to Algiers. He also acted as baggage-master in 1625 for Henrietta Maria's journey from Paris to her wedding at Canterbury. The younger Tradescant voyaged to America and together they are credited with introducing the lilac, acacia, Oriental plane and many other trees and shrubs into Britain. Little remains of the Tradescants' gardens at St Augustine's, but their botanic garden at South Lambeth is now the Museum of Domestic Gardening, while their numerous curiosities from around the world formed the original collection of the Ashmolean Museum at Oxford.

From the Abbey the visitor can take one of two routes, that closest to the pilgrims' path following around to the two Abbey gates. The gatehouses date from the 14th century, both with octagonal turrets and battlements. The Cemetery Gate has been blocked in but the more imposing Great Gate or

21 *The Great Gateway or Fyndon Gate to St Augustine's Abbey and, later, the King's House. In 1625, Charles I and his French bride Henrietta Maria stayed in the Gateway Chamber on their wedding night. On the restoration of the monarchy in 1660, Charles II spent his first night on English soil as king here*

Fyndon Gate (**21**), built under Abbot Thomas Fyndon between 1300 and 1309, is still complete. This handsome two-storeyed building is a fine example of the Decorated Gothic style in the richly panelled surfaces of the upper storey and turrets.

By the 19th century parts of the King's House had fallen into ruin and the rest had become part of a brewery and pleasure grounds. Through the efforts of A.J.B. Beresford-Hope and Edward Coleridge the buildings were restored and converted into St Augustine's College, a missionary college. The 19th-century buildings in the mid-Gothic style by William Butterfield are deliberately monastic in character and incorporate some of the Abbey ruins. From Lady Wooton's Green, outside, there are fine views connecting the college with the two major ecclesiastical elements of Canterbury: to the east, the

Abbey, and in particular the Fyndon Gateway; to the west, the Cathedral, behind the city wall and one of its bastions. The Green itself establishes an almost axial link between Augustine's two great foundations. The remains of the Roman Queningate in the city wall remind us of Bede's story of the conversion of the English. It was through this gateway that Queen Bertha passed each day, going to and from the little Church of St Martin's, during her long vigil of 35 years.

From the Abbey one can alternatively follow **Ivy Lane** (**22**), with its timber-framed medieval ranges, a fine 15th-century Wealden hall, 18th-century cottages, Victorian terraces and some strikingly modern building, all haphazardly mixed together, affording an interesting link between Longport and the city centre.

22 This 15th-century Wealden Hall house is part of a range of houses in Ivy Lane with exposed timber framing

A Pilgrim's path from the West

The band of 29 pilgrims immortalised by Geoffrey Chaucer in the *Canterbury Tales* journeyed from the Tabard Inn at Southwark, London, to the shrine of St Thomas, a journey of four days. Their ambling pace, known as 'the Canterbury gallop', has since passed into our vocabulary as 'cantering'. Their pilgrim bells gave the name to a flower, the Canterbury bell. Although they journeyed with every devotion, some were intent on amusement and recreation. Story-tellers, jugglers and minstrels beguiled the way, so that, 'every town they came through, what with the noise of their singing, and with the sound of their piping, and with the barking of the dogs after them, they made more noise than if the king came there with all his clarions and many other minstrels'.

The final stage of their journey took them to the village of Harbledown, which Chaucer refers to as 'Bob-up-and-down', but the name seems likely to be taken from the cultivation of herbs on the hillsides around, whence 'Herbal down'. In 1084 Archbishop Lanfranc founded **St Nicholas' Hospital (23)** for the care of lepers, out of which have grown the **almshouses (24)** clustered around the tiny Norman church. Nearby is a well of clear water known as the Black Prince's Well. Here Chaucer's pilgrims told their last story and here, at Harbledown, as they came over the ridge and down from the high ground the pilgrims had their first view of the city.

The modern visitor can follow the path of Chaucer's pilgrims through the city, starting at the top of St Dunstan's Street and finishing at the Cathedral. The walk takes in some of the most historic streets, inns, houses, hospices and parish churches of Canterbury, some of which were already ancient in Chaucer's time.

St Dunstan's Street, despite the pressure of traffic, still provides the most historically impressive and architecturally interesting approach to the old walled city. Many of the fine period buildings exhibit medieval features and the building line of the north-east side from St Dunstan's Church down to the massive Westgate Towers remains little changed from the 13th century.

St Dunstan's Church, of flint and stone, was founded in the 11th century, probably by Lanfranc; but much of the building, including the crenellated tower, dates from the later-medieval period. Here Henry II dismounted in 1174 before walking barefoot to the Cathedral as penance for the murder of Becket. St Dunstan's Church is best known for its association with Henry VIII's chancellor, St Thomas More, as, after his execution, his daughter, Margaret Roper, brought his head to rest in the family vault of the Roper Chapel. Nearby the 16th-century brick Roper Gateway, recently restored, is the only surviving part of the former residence of the Roper family.

OVERLEAF

23 *The church of the leper's hospital of St Nicholas of Harbledown. In 1174 on his way to do penance for the murder of Thomas of Becket, Henry II halted here and ordered that a gift of twenty marks a year be given to the leper hospital. Today the gift is still paid to the Harbledown almshouses (24)*

At the lower end of **St Dunstan's Street** (**25**), 13 successive gables of buildings can be counted, all more than four hundred years old. No. 71, 'The House of Agnes', is a prominent example of a 16th-century timber-framed house, with the addition of three leaded 17th-century bay windows to the first floor and two 18th-century bays to the ground floor. The name is associated with the character Agnes Whitfield in Dickens' novel *David Copperfield*. Further along, on the opposite side of the street, is the Falstaff Hotel. It retains its early 15th-century form; its function was to accommodate pilgrims who arrived at the city after the gates were closed at night. Among its many interesting features are the 17th-century bay windows on the first floor, and the elaborate 18th-century wrought iron bracket supporting the inn sign.

The **West Gate** (**26**), completed in 1381, consists of two 60-foot circular towers enclosing the gateway and a chamber used until 1829 as a prison for criminals and condemned persons. Situated on the river, the gateway was complete with drawbridge and portcullis, arrow slit windows and gunports – the earliest example of gunports in England. The West Gate now serves as a museum, showing arms and armour, and access to the roof provides splendid views over the rooftops of Canterbury. Next to it, in a lovely setting by the river, stands Holy Cross Church, built in 1380 by Archbishop Simon Sudbury. It had previously existed as a chapel over an earlier West Gate. Since 1972 it has served as the council chamber for Canterbury City Council.

25 *Timber-framed houses in upper St Dunstan's Street. The cottages in brick or 'mathematical tile' (above) are outwardly 18th-century, but the façade, as commonly found in Canterbury, conceals a medieval core*

26 *The West Gate and Guildhall Council Chamber viewed from the banks of the Stour*

St Peter's Street is one of the city's main arteries, leading directly into the High Street and to the very centre of the historic city. Fortunately the vast numbers of visitors and shoppers crowding into these busy streets are now better accommodated than they used to be, thanks to the pedestrianisation of much of the central area. St Peter's Street is full of architectural and historic interest. Alterations made in the 18th and 19th centuries to the façades of many buildings and modern shop fronts disguise medieval constructions, but projecting upper floors, jettied timber frames and tile-hung gables reveal their true age and character.

Standing back from the busy street, **St Peter's Church** (**27**) is believed to occupy the site of a former Roman church and was perhaps rebuilt by

27 St Peter's Church, partly concealed from St Peter's Street

28 *The Old Weavers'
House (1507), viewed
from the King's Bridge.
The 'ducking stool' is
visible beyond*

St Augustine in Saxon times: the bell tower incorporates Roman tiles and
Saxon corner stones. The present church reveals its Norman phase in the
rounded arch at the end of the north arcade; nearby stands a fine Norman
font. The nave dates from the 12th century, the north aisle having been added
in the 14th century. Early 14th-century stained glass can be seen in the north
window.

On the opposite side of St Peter's Street is the Methodist Church, which
has many associations with John Wesley. The classical exterior has recently
been restored and inside the porch is a table used by Wesley himself. Writing
in 1776, at a time when the Anglican Church had become remote from the
lives of ordinary people, Wesley expressed his hope for a Christian revival:

'Nay, I do not despair even of poor Canterbury; it is not out of God's reach.'

Just two doors away and not to be missed is Cogan House, one of the greatest architectural delights of Canterbury. Concealed behind a shop front and 19th-century red brick façade is an aisled timber-framed hall dating from 1160. The stone walls are over 2 feet thick. Cogan House is one of very few stone houses in Britain surviving from Norman times, unique in Kent and the only urban example of its early medieval type. Its wood panelling, staircases, and stuccoed plaster ceilings are of superb 16th-century Renaissance craftsmanship, while the first floor preserves the 12th-century ambience. It was a private house until the death of its owner, John Cogan, who bequeathed it as a hospital 'for six poor widows of clergymen'. In the 19th century it reverted to private ownership and today it is a restaurant.

The very narrow entrance to All Saints Lane to the left is easily overlooked, but a short detour down the lane leads by a pottery an workshop to All Saints Court. This is a very fine late 15th-century timber-framed building and typical of a Kent merchant's house. As in most old houses in Canterbury the first floor is jettied, that is, supported on projecting beams. This makes the most of a restricted site by giving extra room to the upper floor, and creates a pleasant visual effect. Here the jetty is an exceptional 72 feet long. The carved wood brackets are outstanding, several of them decorated with grotesque animal and human faces.

At the King's Bridge the **Old Weavers House (28)** has five gables overhanging the river, four with oriel windows, and makes a picturesque scene with the weatherboarded and brick riverside buildings and ducking stool. In the 16th century the building was home and workshop to Flemish weavers, driven by religious persecution to seek refuge in England. According to the 18th-century Kent historian Edward Hasted, the weavers 'made choice of Canterbury for their habitation, where they might have the benefit of the river and an easy communication with the metropolis'. Only the front elevation to the street is original; much else has been restored or added in recent times. The present ducking stool is a replica, but there is some evidence that an earlier one was actually used: records of 1660 show it served to punish 'nightwalkers' and 'women of evil fame'.

The Eastbridge Hospital, on the other side of the bridge, is one of the oldest buildings in Canterbury. It was formerly known as St Thomas' Hospital and was founded in 1180 by Edward Fitz Odbold to lodge poor pilgrims after their long journey to Canterbury. Endowed with land and tithes from mills, the hospital succeeded in fulfilling its purpose throughout the Middle Ages. After the Dissolution it was saved to become a school for 20 boys, and by an Act of Parliament in 1584 it was re-established as an almshouse for five elderly men and five elderly women. The present almsfolk are accommodated in the adjacent, modernised 17th-century part that spans the river. They still receive a pension from the original endowment. Admission is free and is through a doorway set in a Norman arch leading to an entrance hall, where the pilgrims were first received. To one side is a small 13th-century chamber now used as a chapel. The steps lead down to the oldest part, a 12th-century stone crypt where pilgrims slept on rushes in the bays. Upstairs a pillared dining hall also dates from the 12th century. On the wall an 800-year-old fresco depicts Christ in Glory. Above the north end of the hall a larger 14th-century chapel and former schoolroom is open only for services. A list of Masters provides an

29 *Greyfriars, the oldest Franciscan building in Britain, is the sole remains of Greyfriars Friary in Canterbury. This view is from the nursery gardens. It is difficult to imagine a more peaceful place within two minutes' walk of the High Street*

unbroken record, even through the late 1340s and early 1380s when the Masters of the Eastbridge did not escape successive waves of plague.

The King's Bridge, spanning the Stour and acting as the link between St Peter's Street and the High Street, has been rebuilt several times on medieval foundations and was widened 10 feet in 1769. It was originally called the Eastbridge, but has been renamed the King's Bridge owing to its proximity to the medieval King's Mill, built by King Stephen (1124–53). The mill was finally demolished in 1800 when the present house on the site was built, but its foundations can be seen at the base of the riverside front.

A short detour to the right along Stour Street leads to the entrance to **Greyfriars** (**29**) and the adjacent Franciscan Gardens. Standing on the island of Binnewith formed by the branches of the Stour, the stone and flint Franciscan dormitory (*c.* 1267) is one of the most picturesque buildings in the old city. (The bucket which hangs suspended over the river under the arch can be hauled up through a trap door.) During the 14th and 15th centuries the dormitory probably housed 35 friars, who were much in demand as confessors, preachers and advisers. Visits to the building can be made by arrangement with the Chapter Office in the Cathedral Precincts.

Further down Stour Street, the Poor Priests' Hospital, which houses Canterbury's 'Time Walk' Heritage Museum, has a magnificent medieval

interior, and tucked away, further along, is the 17th-century Maynard and Cotton Hospital, that is, almshouses, rebuilt on the site of a medieval hospital and chapel.

The amazing **Beaney Institute** (**30**), back in the High Street, is Canterbury's Royal Museum and Public Library, and includes the Buffs Military Museum with its collection of military costume. The Institute was opened in 1897 thanks to the generosity of an Australian, Dr Beaney, who was born in Canterbury. The pseudo-medieval Victorian architecture is vastly out of scale with the much older buildings around.

Queen Elizabeth's Guest Chamber, now used as tea rooms, is so called because it was here in 1573 that Queen Elizabeth I entertained a French

30 *The Beaney Institute in the High Street incorporates the Royal Museum and Art Gallery. Amongst the exhibition pictures are those by one of England's greatest animal painters – Thomas Sydney Cooper, RA*

31 *The Buttermarket for centuries has served as a point of contact between the temporal and the spiritual life of Canterbury. The City of Canterbury War Memorial stands in the centre of the square*

prince, the Duc d'Alençon, with a view to marriage. The Guest Chamber was in the main first floor room and was part of the Crown Inn (1454–1774), which had been one of the principal pilgrims' inns. The fine Elizabethan plaster ceiling was fitted about 1572 and is a splendid example of late-16th-century pargetting. The plasterwork of the exterior façade, with grape vines and figures seated astride barrels and drinking wine, was carried out in the 1660s and recalls the convivial spirit of the Restoration. The entrance to the former coaching yard can be seen to the right of the building.

The view of **Mercery Lane** (see p. 13) from the high Street is one of the most memorable in Canterbury, showing the full medieval character of the city with Christ Church Gate at the end and overhanging buildings almost meeting in the centre. Its name dates back to Solomon, a 12th-century mercer (seller of silks and cloth), who lived on the corner on the site of the building now occupied by Boots. Beneath the basement of Boots a 13th-century vaulted cellar of brick and stone can be visited, and clear water can still be drawn from a well. On the other corner the magnificent stone arcades are the surviving part of the Chequers of Hope Inn. Built for pilgrims in the late 1390s and occupying the whole of the west side of Mercery Lane, the inn is mentioned in the *Canterbury Tales*. The first floor contained individual rooms and the upper storey was a massive dormitory with a hundred beds. Mercery Lane would have been thronged not only with pilgrims but with stalls selling fabrics, brooches, lead pendants of Becket, and bottles of healing water mixed with 'the blood of the saint', among other items that they bought as souvenirs of their visit.

At the far end of Mercery Lane is the **Buttermarket (31)**. The name reminds us that Canterbury has always been a market town for the country around, but compared with the square itself (more than eight hundred years old) it is comparatively recent and replaced the former and more barbarous name of Bullstake only two hundred years ago. For it was here that bulls were baited with dogs, both for sport and, in accordance with belief, to make their flesh more tender. The proximity of Butchery Lane nearby conjures up a gory vision of medieval life that the visitor would little suspect from the appearance of this attractive square today. The Buttermarket is formed on all sides by interesting buildings ranging from the 15th to the 18th centuries. It is the meeting point between the city and Cathedral, and at Christ Church Gate we enter the Precincts.

The Cathedral

Christ Church Gate (**32**) is the main entrance to the Cathedral. It is a dividing point both physically, between the town and the Precincts, and historically, being an example of late Perpendicular Gothic but proclaiming the arrival of the Tudor dynasty in a mass of heraldic shields. Above, angels display shields with the symbols of the Passion. The gate was built to commemorate the marriage of Arthur, the eldest son of Henry VII, to Catherine of Aragon in 1502. Prince Arthur, however, died a few months later and the gateway was not completed until 1521. How different history might have been had Arthur lived to be king to rule with Catherine at his side! Instead Catherine of Aragon, by papal dispensation, was remarried, to Arthur's younger brother, later Henry VIII, and, following the subsequent divorce and its theological complications, the English Church broke from Rome.

The Gate has not always looked as fine as it does today. It suffered badly at the hands of Puritans and in the late 18th century the twin turrets were pulled down, reputedly so that a city Alderman could see the Cathedral clock on the south-west tower from his bank in the High Street. Fortunately, the whole gate was restored in the 1930s by the Friends of Canterbury Cathedral. The splendid ceiling of the great arch is lierne-vaulted, with a boss formed by the Tudor rose. The great oak gates were donated by Archbishop Juxon in 1660. On the north-east pillar two small stone heads are thought to be representations of the hapless Arthur and Catherine.

On 6 October 1990 the Archbishop of Canterbury unveiled the statue of a 'Welcoming Christ' in the central niche of the Christ Church Gate. The original statue was destroyed by the Puritan onslaught during the Civil War and for nearly three hundred and fifty years the niche remained empty. The new bronze figure is the work of the German sculptor Klaus Ringwald, who is famous for his work in cathedrals in southern Germany and beyond. It shows an enthroned Christ, Ruler of the World, with His hands outstretched in welcome. The figure was commissioned by the Friends of Canterbury Cathedral at the time of their Diamond Jubilee in 1987. They required that the statue should 'speak to our age and be a work of spiritual depth and outstanding artistic importance'.

Through the gateway is one of the loveliest views of the Cathedral. The eye is immediately taken upwards by the central tower, called the Bell Harry Tower after the bell Henricus, first referred to in 1228 and therefore considerably older than the tower itself. The masterpiece of the architect John Wastell, the tower was the last part of the Cathedral to be constructed (1497) and, in its sheer, uncomplicated verticality, rising to 235 feet, is one of the most impressive architectural achievements of the English Middle Ages.

At the west end the twin towers, Dunstan and Arundel, seem identical, but are separated in date of construction by four hundred years. The south-west (Dunstan) tower was completed in 1434 and the north-west (Arundel) tower which had survived from the time of Lanfranc, but, as it offended the 19th-century obsession for regularity and the Gothic ideal of Sir Gilbert Scott, it was demolished in 1831. The result is two Gothic towers at the west end. But one pure Romanesque tower does survive, the charming little St Anselm's tower set against St Anselm's Chapel on the south-east of the Cathedral.

The **south-west porch** (**33**) was built in 1424, possibly to commemorate the Battle of Agincourt (1415). The statues of Ethelbert and Bertha to the side, and Archbishops Augustine, Lanfranc, Anselm and Cranmer above, are 19th-century additions. On entering the visitor is immediately impressed by the height and beauty of the nave, the masterpiece of Henry Yevele, constructed between 1373 and 1406 and one of the finest examples of early Perpendicular architecture. Whichever way one looks, whether down the nave at the rows of tall, slender columns or upward at the beautiful lierne-vaulted roof, this lovely building has a marvellous sense of airy spaciousness. 80 feet above the floor, a marvellous sense of airy spaciousness is given by this

32 *The rich ornamentation on Christ Church Gate commemorates the Tudors and, in particular, the ill-fated marriage of Henry VIII's elder brother Arthur to Catherine of Aragon*

52

OVERLEAF

34 *The Cathedral font in black and white marble with classical figures and a fantastic cover caused outrage to the 17th-century puritans*

35 *The Pulpitum, showing the figures of Henry IV and (right) Henry VI*

lovely building. The aisles, which appear even loftier in proportion, are nine bays long and were built on the exact lines of the earlier nave created by Lanfranc.

The glorious west window contains some of the oldest stained glass in the Cathedral. The lower half consists of 13 figures from the original 12th-century sequence depicting the genealogy of Christ stretching back to Adam, as in St Luke's gospel. The genealogy originally consisted of 88 figures set in the clerestory of the choir; in the late 18th century the surviving 45 figures were relocated in various places around the Cathedral. The largest collections are here in the west window (13 figures) and in the great window of the south-west transept (24 figures).

In the lower row the central panel, 'Adam Delving', is especially vivid, showing Adam stripped to the waist and digging the soil, condemned to live by the sweat of his brow. Above, the array of kings and archbishops dates from the late 14th century. The association of kings, prophets, patriarchs and saints, although contrived by an arrangement of the 18th century, reinforces the theme of the universal ancestry of Adam and the divine origin of all authority.

36 *The fine pulpit in the nave was built in 1398*

In the nave, one outstanding feature is the marble font (*c.* 1636), which was rescued from the Puritans and, with the monarchy, restored in 1660. With its huge cover, pulley and chain, the font (**34**) is an elaborate monument to the High Church Anglicanism of Charles I's Archbishop Laud and to the loving care of the 17th-century Cathedral archivist, William Somner, who was responsible for saving it.

Among the monuments that line the walls of the aisles are some fine Elizabethan and Jacobean figures on the north side, including the Hales tomb (1596), depicting a burial at sea, and the portrait bust of the court composer Orlando Gibbons, who wrote the music for Charles I's wedding and whose memorial is placed, appropriately, next to the organ.

The focal point of the nave is the elaborately carved stone screen or **pulpitum** (**35**) (*c.* 1450), the finest work of the master mason Richard Beke (died 1458), at the top of the steps at the entrance to the choir. The figures of the six kings were made for the screen and were deliberately intended to extol the lineage of the Lancastrians and to legitimise their usurpation. Framed by the great Henry V and his son Henry VI to the left and right are the youthful Richard II, Ethelbert (holding the Cathedral), Edward the Confessor (the patron saint of the Lancastrians), and Henry IV. The screen itself frames the view of the choir and Trinity Chapel, and – once upon a time – the shrine of St Thomas. Beneath the Bell Harry Tower, look up to see at a great height John Wastell's **crossing vault** (**37**) (*c.* 1509), one of the most beautiful in Europe

37 *Fan vaulting in the Bell Harry Tower, 'the noblest tower in Christendom'; viewed from the nave steps directly beneath*

and the forerunner of Wastell's best-known vaults at King's College, Cambridge.

The south-west transept was built after the nave. Its magnificent south window contains an incomparable display of 12th-century glass, including 24 patriarchal figures from the dispersed genealogy of Christ. These include the figure of Methusaleh (Matusale) in the lower row, his great age suggested by the way he rests his chin on his right hand, his left hand clutching the arm of his throne.

St. Michael's chapel, also the work of Richard Beke, is a richly decorated memorial to Lady Margaret Holland (died 1439) and her two husbands. She was at the centre of the munificent Beaufort family who financed the building of much of the nave. Such is the power of money that Lady Holland arranged for her magnificent alabaster tomb and chapel to supplant those of Archbishop Stephen Langton, one of England's most distinguished archbishops and author of Magna Carta. Langton's tomb was removed to the east of the chapel, where, to this day, his head lies within but his feet protrude outside the Cathedral wall. The chapel is hung with military flags and is dedicated to the memory of the fallen, especially those of the Buffs. Here each day a soldier comes at 11 a.m. and in a short ceremony formally turns over a page of the Book of Remembrance.

The place of Becket's martyrdom, for centuries the most venerated spot in the Cathedral is in the north-west transept. Although the adjacent Lady Chapel (1448), which contains magnificent, large-scale fan vaulting, has transformed this part of the Cathedral since Becket's time, much has been left untouched, including some original Lanfranc work and the floor, which remains lower than the corresponding south side of the transept.

The murder of Becket in Canterbury Cathedral is the subject of great historical and literary works, but there can be no substitute for the actual words spoken by the Archbishop on that fateful Tuesday, 29 December 1170. 'I will not have the Church made a Castle', Becket declared as he ordered the monks to open the door. Then, in answer to the accusations of the four knights, he said 'I am no traitor, but the Archbishop and Priest of God.' With only the Saxon monk Grim at his side and kneeling in prayer, Becket murmured, 'Into thy hands, O Lord, I commend my spirit.' After the second blow Becket uttered his last mortal words, 'For the name of Jesus, and the defence of the Church, I am willing to die.' (**38**)

On the wall a simple plaque commemorates a great occasion of more recent times: 'In this place, hallowed by the martyrdom of Thomas Becket, 29 December 1170, Pope John Paul II and Robert Runcie, Archbishop of Canterbury, knelt together in prayer, 29 May 1982.'

The glass of the huge north window of the transept, the work of William Neve (1482), depicts Edward IV, his Queen, Elizabeth Woodville, and the whole royal family, including at the left the tragic princes, Richard, Duke of York and Edward, Prince of Wales, who were murdered in the Tower.

Entry into the choir, up the stairs taken by countless pilgrims to the place of Becket's shrine, is marked stylistically by a transition to the earlier Gothic work of William of Sens (1175–8), succeeded by William the Englishman (1179–94). It was on 9 September 1174 that the eastern part of the Cathedral was burnt down, an event well documented by Gervase, a contemporary monk. The fire had broken out in the Burgate and, unnoticed by local townsfolk, a few sparks penetrated the Cathedral roof between the wooden rafters. As the fire caught beneath the roof the lead began to melt with catastrophic effect. The crypt, outside walls and surrounding towers, however, survived the blaze and when the monks commissioned the French architect, William of Sens, to restore their cathedral they implored him to save what remained of the old choir. The result is a Gothic interior within a Romanesque shell. Among the earlier parts preserved are the two parallel Romanesque towers and chapels of St Andrew and St Anselm, the latter with its 800-year-old **fresco of St Paul** (**39**) throwing a viper into a fire. In the south choir aisle a portion of Norman rounded arcading has a small pointed arch chiselled out at the end, as if for demonstration purposes to persuade the doubting monks to rebuild the rest of the choir in the new, Gothic style.

The architecture of William of Sens is closely linked with Sens Cathedral and this is evident in the twin circular and octagonal columns, the Corinthian capitals and the sexpartite vaulting system (**40**). All are characteristic of the earliest Gothic in France and Canterbury Cathedral also shares this link with Notre Dame in Paris, which had been begun in 1163. In September 1178, when William of Sens had completed the fifth row of columns and was working high on the great vault of the crossing, the wooden scaffolding collapsed and he fell 50 feet to the floor. In great pain he carried on through the following winter, directing operations from his sick-bed, but, 'perceiving that he derived no benefit from the physicians, gave up the work, and crossing the sea, returned to his home in France'.

40 *Detail of William de Sens' Choir arcade*

The monks turned to another architect named William, 'in workmanship of many kinds acute and honest', and the English William was to prove himself as innovative as the Frenchman. By 1178–80 St Thomas was a cult figure, pilgrims were flocking to Canterbury and the visit of the French King Louis VII in 1179 established the reputation of the martyr on an international scale. The thought of glorifying the Cathedral by constructing a great shrine above the congested crypt was behind the decision to transfer Becket's tomb directly above to form the centrepiece of a new chapel. This was the achievement of William the Englishman, who raised the easternmost part of the Cathedral to create the Trinity Chapel, the perfect setting for Becket's tomb, and the beautiful Corona.

For the visitor the transition to 12th-century Gothic is marked by the continually rising flights of stairs. The choir is lifted above the two-centuries-later nave; the presbytery is higher than the choir; the level rises again with a flight of 16 steps, worn by the knees of three and a half centuries of pilgrims, to the **Trinity Chapel** (**41**). This was the climax of the pilgrimage, where, above the high altar, the shrine of Becket's tomb was covered with dazzling gold and jewels. In the Trinity Chapel are the remains of a marble pavement in *opus alexandrinum*, said to be gift from Pope Innocent III, which surrounded the shrine in a geometrical pattern flanked by 36 roundels of virtues and vices, the months of the year and signs of the zodiac. Almost as old is St Augustine's Chair, probably of the 13th century, in which each successive archbishop is enthroned.

The stained-glass windows of the choir clerestory (**42**) are a Victorian reproduction of the original genealogy of Christ which had been taken down in the 18th century and repositioned about the Cathedral. (It begins with 'Adam delving' at the north-west end of the choir.) But the choir aisles display by far the oldest and loveliest large collection of stained glass in England. In the north choir aisle the 12th-century 'Theological' windows, a form of Bible for the unlearned, reflect the medieval practice of associating events in the Old and New Testaments. The Nativity scene, for instance, of Mary and the infant Jesus, with shepherds and Magi bearing gifts, is

41 The Choir looking east. The aisle pillars, taller and slimmer than in earlier Norman churches, support black Purbeck marble shafts, and their carving is reflected in the capitals of the columns below the clerestory from which the roof vaults spring. The eastern part of the Choir, Trinity Chapel and the Corona—the circular chamber at the easternmost end which creates an effect of depth and distance—were the work of William the Englishman

paralleled by Solomon receiving gifts from the Queen of Sheba, and the brothers of Joseph bringing him money for corn in Egypt.

The subjects of the 12 principal windows in the Trinity Chapel, the **Miracle Windows**, relate to the life and posthumous miracles of St Thomas and were painted within a decade of his death. One of the best-known stories (north 6th window) is of Bobby (Robertulus), who fell into the Medway. We see him falling into the mud, his friends running for help, and his mother dragging him out alive, thanks to a miracle. The small Geoffrey of Winchester is in the 12th window: a wall collapses on his cradle, his mother faints and a servant throws water over her, another servant clears away the rubble and finds the cradle in pieces, but Geoffrey is unhurt. The top circle of the fifth window has a very precious fragment, showing us the golden shrine of Becket as it was in 1220. The windows in the **Corona** (**43**), so named because it contained a relic of the crown of Becket's head, have 13th-century glass, illustrating prophetic scenes from the Old Testament and, in the central panel, the Crucifixion, Resurrection and Ascension of Christ.

42 *Clerestory windows in the Trinity Chapel: this sequence depicts the life of Christ*

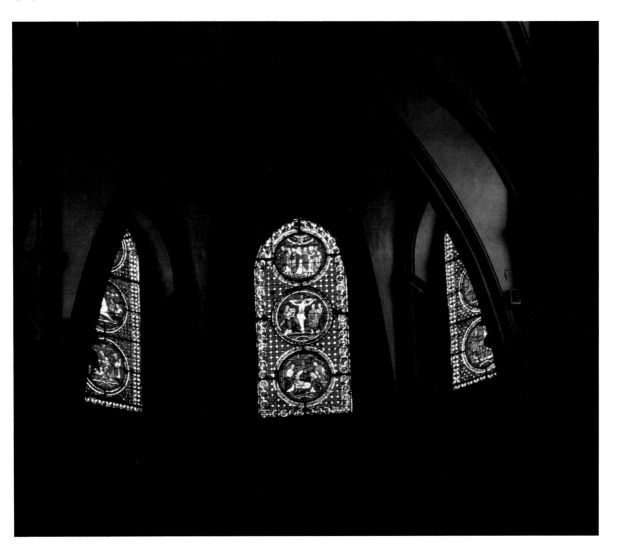

Around the choir runs the stone screen of Prior Henry of Eastry (1304), the only prior to be accorded a monument (it stands in the south choir aisle). At the west end of the choir the carved oak stalls used by the dean and chapter are more recent, dating from 1682, but the rest of this marvellous building is a treasure-house of Early English Gothic, built on and into a Romanesque structure. This remarkable combination of architectural styles came about as a result of the great fire four years after Becket's death.

Among the famous tombs, perhaps the most remarkable is Archbishop Chichele's (died 1443) (**44**). He had it made in his lifetime with two figures: his effigy as archbishop in his full pontificals is above, and below is a figure of him as a corpse. In the Corona are monuments of the infamous Cardinal Pole (died 1558), archbishop under Mary Tudor and responsible for many burnings of Protestants, and the more recent and gentle figure of Archbishop Frederick Temple (died 1902), kneeling in prayer. To the south side of the high altar, the high vaulted canopy over the tomb chest of Archbishop Sudbury (died 1381) was designed to allow sunlight to pass through the monument to the High Altar. Sudbury was murdered by a mob in the Peasants' Revolt; the decapitated body was buried with a canon ball to represent his head. Perhaps the finest stone monument in the Cathedral is the tomb of Archbishop Stratford (died 1348) with its wealth of early Perpendicular detail.

The only monarch to rest in the Cathedral, Henry IV (1367–1413), has a spectacular double tomb, shared with his second wife. Jean of Navarre (died 1437); they are represented by lavish alabaster effigies. Henry IV's tiny chapel has some of the earliest fan vaulting in the Cathedral. Across the Trinity Chapel on the south side is the most splendid memorial of a medieval prince in England, that of **Edward, the Black Prince** (1330–76) (**45**), perhaps so called from a suit of black armour. He rests here in full armour, his head upon a helmet, hands joined in his last prayer and on his feet the likeness of the spurs he won at Crecy. The ostrich feathers, according to tradition, were won at Crecy from the blind King of Bohemia, and they with the motto on the shields, 'Ich diene' ('I serve'), are still the badge of the Prince of Wales. The story is told that after the victory at Poitiers the Black Prince stood behind the captured French King John at dinner and served him as an attendant. Reverence to age and authority, and generosity to the fallen enemy were the hallmarks of chivalry, but to the French 'Le Prince Noir', the Prince of Darkness, earned his name for more sinister reasons: at Limoges in 1371 he gave orders for every woman and child to be slaughtered. In the south choir aisle are displayed the achievements borne at his funeral: the prince's coat, shield, scabbard, gauntlets and helmet.

The entrance to the crypt is by a Norman arch and it is into the Norman world that one enters. This is the largest and oldest Romanesque crypt of any English cathedral, built mostly between 1096 and 1107, but containing some earlier work. The vigorously animated carvings on the capitals of the pillars form the finest collection of Norman sculpture in England.

The crypt contains a remarkable silver exhibition, a collection of items belonging to the Cathedral and to local churches. Among the more unusual treasures are a Saxon pocket sundial in gold and silver, the oldest pocket-watch in the English speaking world, a mazer bowl containing a crystal that according to tradition was attached to one of Becket's garments, and a crosier ornamented with antique gems, found in the tomb of Archbishop Hubert Walter.

In the centre of the crypt is the beautiful Chapel of Our Lady, with marvellously delicate stonework. It was built by the Black Prince in the 14th century and was intended to be his resting place. The eastern part of the crypt (**46**) was built to support William the Englishman's extensions to the Cathedral, added after 1179 to contain Becket's shrine.

On the south side of the crypt, St Gabriel's Chapel has a 12th-century fresco, depicting Christ surrounded by the angelic host. Here too are some of the finest carved capitals. The Black Prince's Chantry, a Norman structure covered by some fine Perpendicular stonework, is still used as a French Huguenot chapel. On the north side of the crypt, Holy Innocents Chapel has two exceptionally beautiful decorated Romanesque pillars. To this exquisite chapel, deep in the most ancient part of the Cathedral, people have brought their children for centuries to be blessed and baptised.

47 *The Cathedral viewed from the Green Court*

The Precincts

Canterbury Cathedral, like many English cathedrals, was founded with a monastery, which formed the Priory of Christ Church and became, until its dissolution in the reign of Henry VIII, one of the largest Benedictine monasteries in the country. It is unusual in that the monastery was not situated to the south of the Cathedral to take best advantage of sunlight, but to the north. The reason had much to do with water. The 12th-century map of the waterworks, drawn up by the enterprising Prior Wibert (1153–67), shows how water was piped from pure springs which existed to the north of Canterbury; the north side of the Cathedral was the best place to benefit from the supply of fresh drinking water.

In the Middle Ages the abbot of Christ Church was also archbishop of Canterbury, and occasionally the monks made a point of insisting on their right to elect the abbot/archbishop. For six years in the turbulent reign of King John (1199–1215), the entire monastic community was exiled to France for defying the king over the choice of archbishop. To this day in any vacancy of the archbishopric its spiritual powers pass to the Chapter of Canterbury. The archbishop himself enters the Cathedral as the escorted guest of the Chapter. In practice the archbishop/abbots of the Middle Ages had little time for the affairs of the monastery, so a prior was appointed to exercise the abbot's functions, hence the Priory of Christ Church.

The Precincts have not always been quiet and peaceful. In the days of the Priory scenes of great commotion were not uncommon. In 1189, before Archbishop Baldwin died as a crusader in the Holy Land, he attempted to reform Christ Church Priory. The monks resisted and behaved so badly towards their prior, who had been imposed on them by the archbishop, that he had to escape from the Precincts through a sewer. (It suited his character, the chronicler wrote!) Tired of the monks, the archbishop decided to establish a rival monastery just outside the city at St Stephen's, endowing it with the Cathedral monks' own property. Citizens took sides in the dispute and tremendous fights ensued. The archbishop's party included some of the monks' servants, such as William the Watchman, John the Cook and Godefrid the Baker. Petitions to Rome resulted in the Pope putting an end to the plan. The year 1327 saw a clear-cut struggle between city and Priory, owing to the King's command that the city of Canterbury provide and equip 20 horsemen for the Scottish war. The monks refused to subscribe, claiming exemption, and in reprisal angry citizens resolved to prevent pilgrims entering the Cathedral, to strip any monk stark naked and to loot Becket's shrine. Of these ancient rivalries between city and Cathedral, a reminder

48 *The Son of Man by David McFall (1989)*

survives in that the Chapter does not allow the Lord Mayor to have his mace carried erect within the Precincts.

Along the south side of the Cathedral the simple landscape of mown grass, trees and paths provides a pleasant, open setting for some magnificent views. At the east end stands the modern statue of Christ (**56**) completed by David McFall shortly before his death and placed here in 1989. The large rectangular area of grass beyond, known as the Oaks, was once the monastic fish pond, and on the far side holes which housed beehives can be seen in the brick wall. The old round-arched Cemetery Gate that leads into the War Memorial Garden was built about 1160 and originally stood at a point further west. The eastern boundary of the War Memorial Garden is dominated by the city wall and a large bastion converted into a chapel. The Queningate leads through the city wall and out towards the 14th-century Fyndon Gate of St Augustine's, the great rival of Christ Church Priory in the Middle Ages.

Rounding the east end of the Cathedral brings into view the ruins of the 12th-century **Infirmary Chapel** (**49**) and, to the east, one of the large houses

49 *The ruins of the Infirmary Chapel and (beyond) the flint wall of the Cathedral choir boys' house*

OVERLEAF

50 *The Corona and Bell Harry Tower are nicely juxtaposed in this view westwards from the Kent War Memorial Garden. The gate (left) was built about 1160 and once stood further to the west as the entrance to the monks' burial ground*

in which the monks accommodated important persons staying at the monastery. The house, known as **Meister Omers** (**51**), was built about 1220 and is named after Master Omer, a monastic bailiff. The house was greatly extended in 1395 by Prior Chillenden to become the refectory for the prior's most important guests, among whom were King Edward IV, who held a Great Council here in 1453, and Elizabeth I. Meister Omers is also the location of an Elizabethan mystery. In 1568 the French Cardinal Odet de Coligny, who had become a Protestant and fled the French wars of religion, died in mysterious circumstances while lodging here. There was suspicion of murder by means of a poisoned apple and the crime was reputedly confessed to some years later by a servant. Meister Omers is now a boarding house of the King's School.

Linacre House, named after Thomas Linacre (1460–1524), and also part of the school, is situated beyond and can be seen through the ruins of the Infirmary Chapel. Linacre was physician to Henry VIII, Mary Tudor and Cardinal Wolsey, and founded the Royal College of Physicians. Next comes

51 Meister Omers. The *flint-dressed-with-stone chimneys and gabled semi-dormers contribute to the 19th-century exterior, but the house has many medieval features, including a huge fireplace more than 17ft wide in the old kitchen*

74

the Choir School – the other school within the Precincts – whose east wall, visible from the Linacre forecourt, is considered the finest flintwork in Kent. The interior contains the Infirmary Dining Hall. The ruins opposite are those of the monastic Infirmary. Beyond, attached to the Cathedral, is one of the Romanesque legacies of Prior Wibert: the Cathedral Treasury, whose barred windows (original) proclaim its function.

Passing through the Infirmary Cloister and beyond the **Dean's Steps** (**52**) we encounter another architectural gem, the octagonal **Water Tower** (**53**) (*c*. 1160), built by Prior Wibert for the monastic waterworks. It was the

53 *The Water Tower (12th-century) and (right) part of the Cathedral Library reconstructed after wartime bomb damage*

terminal point of the piped supply to the monastery, and from the upper part water was distributed all around the monastery. It is best seen from the adjoining garden, the monastic herbarium or herb garden. From here the remains of the vaults of the enormous Great Dormitory can also be seen to the west. Measuring 148 feet by 78 feet, it was the sleeping quarters for 150 monks. Part of the building is now the Cathedral Library, rebuilt after World War II, when the dormitory received a direct hit. An 11th-century vaulted tunnel (**54**) passing under the former dormitory connects the Infirmary Cloister with the Great Cloister.

54 *The passage to the Infirmary Cloister passes under the site of the Dormitary, much of which is now taken up by the new Cathedral Library*

The Great Cloister (1397–1414), mainly Perpendicular in style but with some fine Norman work and beautiful Early English arcading in the north walk, constituted the heart of the monastery. Together with the completion of the Cathedral nave and Chapter House, the rebuilding of the cloister was undertaken by Prior Thomas Chillenden (1399–1411), who brought about a thorough reformation of the Priory. It takes an effort of imagination today to visualise the daily life of the monks, but walking around the cloister one passes the Norman entrance to the dormitory (now the Cathedral Library) on the east, the Refectory and beyond that the kitchens to the north, the Archbishop's Palace in the north-west corner, and the Cellarer's Range or main stores on the west. The hole in the wall by the north-west corner was the Rota or serving hatch for ale, which the monks took as they passed by. On the

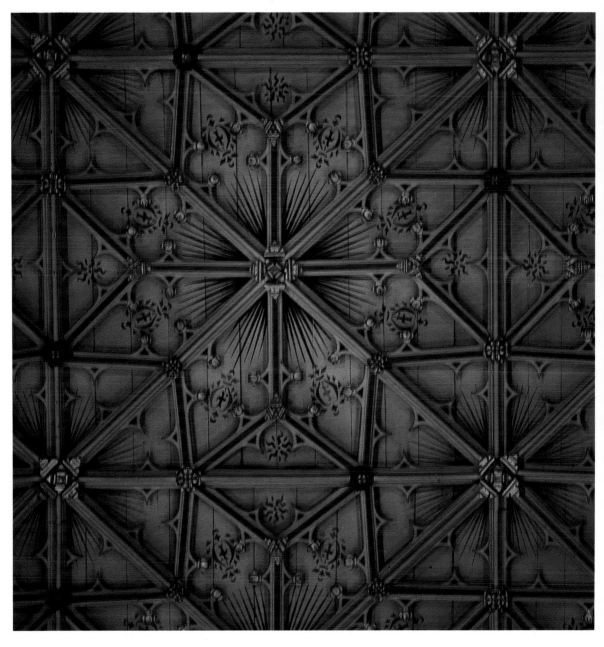

bosses of the lierne-vaulted ceiling are the heraldic shields (**55**), 864 in all, of the donors who had helped to build the Cathedral – a medieval subscription list – which probably constitutes the largest collection of heraldry to survive from the Middle Ages. The cloister door in the south-east corner leads into the Cathedral and the place where Becket was murdered.

Another art form of past generations is the scratched inscriptions, initials and footprints to be seen all around the cloisters, especially in the south passage. One of these 18th-century 'footprints' is initialled C.A., probably referring to Charles Abbot (1762–1832), a King's School boy, who later became Lord Tenterden, Lord Chief Justice of England.

55 *Coats of arms in the vaulting of the Great Cloister*

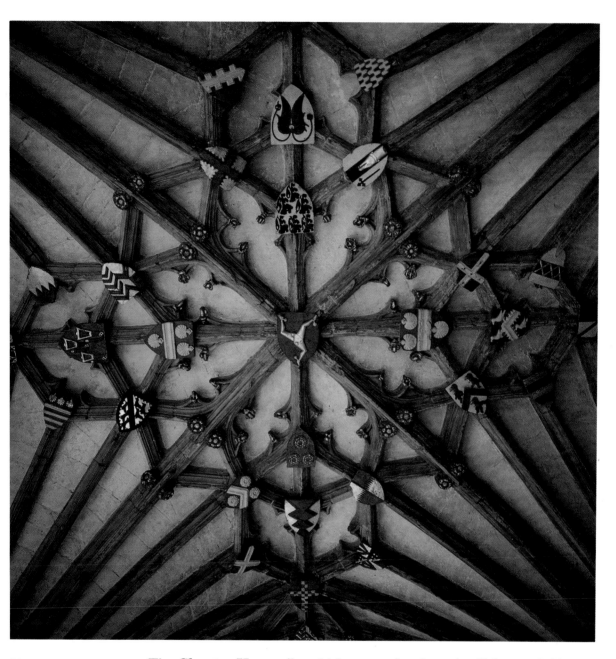

56 *A detail of the splendid Chapter House roof showing the lattice-work*

The **Chapter House** (late 14th century), where the 'Priors and Chapter did meet to consult about the affairs of this Church and Monastery', is roofed with an elaborately decorated wooden wagon-vault (**56**). The grand throne at the far end was used by the prior, with the monks occupying the low stone seats around, and here they assembled for all important meetings as well as for the routine matters of the day. This was the setting of the first performances of T.S. Eliot's drama on the death of Becket, *Murder in the Cathedral*. More recently, it was here that Prime Minister Margaret Thatcher and President Mitterand of France signed the treaty for the construction of the Channel Tunnel.

57 *The appropriately named Dark Entry*

58 *The Chapter House Window. The Victorian stained glass depicts archbishops and monarchs*

Returning to the Infirmary Cloister and turning left past some slender 12th-century spiral columns one enters the aptly named **Dark Entry** (**57**), supposed to be haunted by a ghost. The story of the ghost of Nell Cook is told in the *Ingoldsby Legends* by the Rev. R.H. Barham (1840), where it is called the 'King's Scholar's Story'. The legend goes that in the days of Henry VIII a cook named Nell, employed by a canon of the Cathedral, so resented the presence in the household of a young woman alleged to be the priest's niece that she poisoned them both. She is said to have been walled up in the Dark Entry, which her spirit is supposed to haunt on Fridays at 9 p.m.: 'It fears me quite – it's Friday night! – and then Nell Cook hath power!'

Green Court and the King's School

The Prior Selling Gate (15th century) links two worlds both physically and metaphorically. The passage and cloisters behind are intimate and small scale, but beyond the gateway the space bursts wide open in the **Green Court** (**59**) and here the ecclesiastical world of the Cathedral mingles with and gives way to the educational world of the King's School. The two are intimately linked, sharing the Precincts and built on a common foundation with the same coat of arms. The blue and white shield appears on buildings throughout the Precincts, inscribed with the Greek initials I X of Jesus Christ.

59 *The Green Court, once the business centre of the monastery and now the nucleus of the King's School*

Across the Green Court is a range of 14th-century grey flint buildings with steeply pitched tiled roofs, which once contained the monastic brewery, granary and stables. The east side of the Green Court is dominated by the **Deanery** (**60**). The building in part dates back to the 16th century and, in its older portions, to the 13th century, and is the stateliest of English deaneries. It also shows considerable evidence of repair and rebuilding, not least due to bomb damage in World War II. A remarkable feature of its furnishings is a series of contemporary portraits of the deans of Canterbury from the Reformation. From the time of the Civil War, when a large part of the Archbishop's Palace was destroyed, until 1899, when the present Palace was built, it was the custom of the archbishop, when at Canterbury, to reside at the Deanery as guest of the dean.

60 *The Deanery, much repaired and rebuilt through the centuries. The flint, castellated tower is 15th-century and the brick, central portion is a restored (following bomb damage) 16th-century building*

The first Dean of Canterbury, when the monastery was dissolved and a dean and chapter replaced the prior and monastic body, was Nicholas Wotton (1542–67), the only dean to have a tomb in the Cathedral choir. In our own century three of the best-known deans were George Bell (1924–29), one of the 20th century's greatest churchmen; Dick Sheppard (1929–31), one of the 20th century's greatest communicators; and Dr Hewlett-Johnson (1931–63), one of the most controversial figures in the Church of England.

George Bell, Dean of Canterbury for five years, left to become Bishop of

Chichester, with his own and the Cathedral's reputation greatly enhanced. He would almost certainly have succeeded William Temple as archbishop of Canterbury in 1944 but for his views in World War II against mass bombing of German civilians and his attempts to work with the anti-Nazi elements within Germany itself. At Canterbury he was responsible for making the Cathedral more accessible to visitors and for promoting the arts. Dean Bell started the Friends of Canterbury Cathedral, which commissioned John Masefield, the Poet Laureate, to write a nativity play, *The Coming of Christ*, with music by Gustav Holst; this was a great innovation in church life and led, in the 1930s, to the commissioning of new plays, including Eliot's *Murder in the Cathedral*. One of Dean Bell's achievements was to restore the ancient tradition of the dean, rather than the archdeacon, enthroning a new archbishop. He stage-managed the enthronement of Archbishop Lang in 1928 in the chair of St Augustine, which was placed in full view at the east end of the nave, where all enthronements have taken place since.

Dick Sheppard was engaged in social work in London when he become a parson. He turned his parish of St Martin's-in-the-Fields into one of London's most famous centres of social work and, despite protests from some clergy, pioneered religious broadcasting. His *The Impatience of a Parson* was published in 1927 and more than a hundred thousand copies of it were sold before his death. One of Sheppard's first actions on arrival at Canterbury was to discard gaiters, much to the dismay of other priests in the Chapter. The Dean's lack of pomposity helped to bring the Cathedral to terms with the 20th century; communicants quadrupled within a year of his arrival, and on Sunday evenings he preached to congregations of two thousand people. Sadly, ill health took its toll and his doctors ordered him to resign, but he continued his social work in London until his death in 1937. When his coffin lay at St Martin's a hundred thousand people passed by. Dick Sheppard is buried in the Cathedral cloisters.

Dr Hewlett-Johnson, known as the Red Dean on account of his pro-Communist views, was a source of constant conflict within the Chapter, the diocese and the wider Church. His visits to Iron Curtain countries, acceptance of the Stalin Peace Prize and avowed Communist sympathies at the height of the Cold War generated much dismay within the Anglican Communion. In 1947 Archbishop Fisher felt obliged to issue a press statement formally dissociating himself from Hewlett-Johnson's views and repeating a warning given by Archbishop Lang ten years before that the Dean should not attempt to speak for the Church beyond the confines of Canterbury Cathedral. On Easter Day 1956, George Malenkov, the former Soviet Prime Minister, had luncheon at the Deanery. Looking out of the window at the Cathedral, he was heard to say, 'You take all this for granted. To me it is all entirely new and wonderful.' A little later the Dean received a furious letter from Archbishop Fisher for bringing an 'unbeliever' into the Cathedral on Easter Day. Later, in 1960, Hewlett-Johnson hung a large notice over the Deanery door bearing the words, 'Christians, Ban Nuclear Weapons'. While the Red Dean aroused many emotions ranging from hostility to enthusiasm, none could criticise his commitment to Canterbury during the war, when he remained in the city throughout despite severe bomb damage to the Deanery and parts of the Precincts. He too is buried in the cloisters.

61 *The Archdeacon's House and, adjoining it, a glimpse of the Pentise*

On the south side of the Green Court are the ruins of the Necessarium or monastic lavatory. This 12th-century structure, containing no fewer than 56 toilet seats and sluiced by channels of waste water from the Water Tower, was well situated next to the Great Dormitory. Larder Gate, once the entrance to the monastic kitchens, fell into ruin after the Reformation but was rebuilt in 1951. The building bears the arms of the King's School and, on account of a sister school at Parramatta, the arms of Australia as well. Next door to Lardergate is the archdeacon's residence (**61**), built *c.* 1400 by Prior Chillenden as guest lodgings. From its iron gate can be seen the Pentise (1393), a wooden covered way for pilgrims passing through to Becket's shrine

which is contemporary with Chaucer's *Canterbury Tales*. The stone wall beyond marks the boundary between the monastery and the former grounds of the Archbishop's Palace. That area is now dominated by the school's Assembly Hall, opened in 1957.

The other buildings of Green Court now all pertain to the school. On the north side the recessed house containing the school's offices is dated 1659 in a brick pattern between the sash windows. It is known as Hodgson's Hall and named after the master who was responsible for the turfing in the 1870s of the Green Court, making it more suitable for cricket. Today it is uneven, owing to the construction of underground shelters during the last war. Beneath the 15th-century archway at the north-east corner two enormous firehooks are attached to the wall. From this side of the Green Court the view of the Cathedral is spectacular, the full length of the Cathedral building appearing in a superb context of open space and monastic buildings.

In the north-west corner, the **Norman Staircase (62)** (*c.* 1153) is another part of Prior Wibert's architectural legacy. It led up to the middle of the Aula Nova or Poor Pilgrims' Hall, built on arches of which three survive. It is reputed to be the only outside Norman staircase in England, and originally it supported another water tower. Prior Wibert also built the rich Green Court Gateway (mid-12th century), which was the main entrance to the monastery. Above it the present Durnford History Library was added by Prior Chillenden about 1400. Beneath and entered by the Norman undercroft is the lovely Memorial Chapel, which includes stained-glass windows commemorating Cardinal Pole and Archbishop Parker, both benefactors of the King's School, albeit implacable opponents of each other. The Chapel is open to visitors during school term.

To the north-west the Mint Yard is so called because from the 7th century the archbishop's mint stood on the site. For centuries the school was located in the Almonry building, which stood on the site now occupied by Mitchinson's House. The Grange was probably the granary of the Archbishop's Palace. The north wall is medieval and represents the boundary of the old palace. The fireplace in the 'Old Grange' belonged to Matthew Parker, the first archbishop of Queen Elizabeth I, and it bears his arms, which also appear over the doorway. The interior staircase dates from the 17th century, and probably came from the Archbishop's Palace when it was demolished by the Puritans.

Around the Mint Yard, School House and Galpin's were built as one house in 1865. Until 1935, Galpin's was the head master's private residence. A monastic prison, used for French prisoners-of-war in the Napoleonic Wars, also existed here. The Mint Yard Gateway itself is Victorian, but the gates come from the Green Court Gateway. **The Old King's School Shop (63)** (1612), outside the Mint Yard Gate and facing it, belonged to Sir John Boys, one time M.P. and Recorder of Canterbury. It is one of the most photographed buildings in the city, picturesque but also very precarious, as the leaning front door indicates.

The King's School: A Brief History

King's is probably the oldest school in the country, if not in the entire world. Education was at the heart of St Augustine's mission to England in 597 and

the establishment of a school would have been part of the foundation of a cathedral and monastery. By the time of Archbishop Theodore (668–90) the school at Canterbury was a model for other schools founded in Saxon times. Theodore, a native of Greece, and the Abbot Hadrian, who had already presided over a monastery at Naples, were products of that Byzantine culture which combined Christian learning with the love of Greek and Roman antiquity. Subsequently the influence of the school went far beyond the boundaries of the kingdom of Kent, carried by students who had come to Canterbury in search of education.

One of the scholars who flocked to Abbot Hadrian's school was Aldhelm, later the first Bishop of Sherborne. Letters that he wrote explain how much he owed to the teaching at Canterbury, especially to Hadrian, 'the venerated teacher of my rude infancy'. Roman law, verse-making, music, arithmetic and astronomy were among the subjects studied. There is also a description of Archbishop Theodore, surrounded by a class of less diligent scholars, 'rending them with the tusk of grammar, like a fierce boar penned in by growling hounds of the Molassian breed'. (Schoolmastering has changed little in its essentials!) Bede records that another scholar of Canterbury to be ordained bishop, St John of Beverley, even remembered some medicine from his studies. The Saint rebuked some attendants for bleeding a sick nun, saying: 'I remember Archbishop Theodore of blessed memory telling how dangerous is bloodletting when the moon is waxing full and the sea is flowing to high tide' (this from the school that later produced the fathers of modern medicine, Linacre and Harvey).

During the Middle Ages, the school, known as the Archbishop's or Almonry School, was re-established by Lanfranc's Charter of 1095, 'both in grammar and in music for the city and its neighbourhood'. A continuous line of head masters is recorded from 1291, but it is also clear that previously ('old old') head masters had exercised jurisdiction 'in all matters affecting the school and the scholars'. One of the now-discontinued medieval customs took place on St Nicholas' Day (6 December), when the boys of the school elected their own Boy Bishop. Wearing this boy-sized cope and mitre, the Boy Bishop walked in procession to the Cathedral, preached a sermon, parodied the other duties of the clergy and generally ruled for the day.

After the suppression of the monastery, King Henry VIII recognized the existence of the school and made it part of the Cathedral foundation by the foundation statute of 1541. The school, now called the King's School, suffered no break in the continuity of its history, for the boys were the same, the head master, John Twyne, was the same and, after a brief period at the south side of the Cathedral, the school was restored to its former location in the Mint Yard. The 1541 charter required the dean and chapter to provide for the maintenance of 'fifty poor scholars' until they had obtained 'a moderate acquaintance with the Latin grammar, and have learned to speak in Latin and to write in Latin'. The statutes contained a warning for the scholars: 'If any of the boys be remarkable for extraordinary slowness or dullness, or for a natural distaste for learning', it is the royal will that 'after much trial he be expelled least as a drone be devour the honey of the bees'.

King's has known some remarkable head masters. John Twyne (1535–1561), a rumbustious character, bridged the transition from monastic school to the refounded King's School and became Mayor of Canterbury in 1554. Twyne adhered to the 'old religion' and in 1553, under the Protestant regime of Edward VI, he was arrested by order of the Regent, the Duke of Northumberland, and held in the Tower of London. On his return to Canterbury Twyne was triumphantly elected Mayor. A few months later the accession of Mary Tudor was threatened by a Kentish knight, Sir Thomas Wyatt, who set himself up at the head of a revolt. Twyne raised guns, ammunition and men in defence of the Catholic Queen and helped to put an end to Wyatt's ambitions.

Twyne was clearly a gifted head master. He persuaded Cardinal Pole to grant the Mint Yard to the school for five hundred years. He was also a distinguished classicist, wrote books on history and scientific phenomena and read just about everything. His religious sympathies, however, were to be his undoing. In 1558 Elizabeth came to the throne and the country became Protestant again. Archbishop Parker wanted to rid King's of its unruly head master and ordered an ecclesiastical visitation of the school (the epithet 'nosey Parker' seems well justified). The inspectors asserted that Twyne was inclined to 'ryot and drunkeness' and his resignation was soon obtained.

Elizabethan and early Stuart Canterbury was, like Canterbury in the days of Archbishop Theodore and Abbot Hadrian, famous for its learning, and it is not surprising that many King's boys caught the Renaissance fever. The best-known Old King's Scholar, Christopher Marlowe (1564–1593), was the son of a shoemaker in the city. Raised in profoundly turbulent times and with a record of brawling in the city streets, Marlowe was always liable to moments of violent temper. His murder in a tavern brawl at Deptford at the early age of 29, in the sinister company of men involved in spying or double-dealing, is one of the famous unsolved mysteries in the history of English Literature. Besides being a brilliant poet and playwright Marlowe seems to have been a government agent. It has even been alleged that he was not murdered, but escaped to the Continent where he continued to write, producing plays generally attributed to Shakespeare. (The inquest verdict that Marlowe died when he attacked a man who acted in self-defence seems more plausible.)

William Harvey (1577–1657), regarded with Thomas Linacre before him as a founder of modern medicine, is best known for the discovery of the circulation of blood, first published in *De Motu Cordis (Of the Heart's Movement)* in 1628. Harvey was also physician to James I and Charles I. John Tradescant the younger (1608–62), who is associated particularly with the gardens of St Augustine's, was another outstanding representative in the quest for knowledge, especially in the field of botanical research. Other Old King's Scholars of the era were Edward Dering, praised by Archbishop Parker as 'the greatest learned man in England', Stephen Gosson, another poet and playwright, who became a Puritan preacher, and Richard Boyle, himself Lord High Treasurer of Ireland and the father of Robert Boyle (an Etonian), the 'father of chemistry' and propounder of Boyle's Law.

In more recent times, eminent King's scholars have included the Victorian critic and essayist Walter Pater (1839–94), the novelists Hugh Walpole (1884–1941) and Somerset Maugham (1874–1965), and Viscount Montgomery (1887–1976), the Allied Commander during World War II. The fictional hero of Dickens' *David Copperfield* received his only useful formal education in the school, with 'the congenial sound of the Cathedral bell hovering over all', while Philip Carey, in Somerset Maugham's *Of Human Bondage*, endured his schooldays here. Maugham's ashes were scattered in the garden near the Norman staircase.

For centuries King's was a small grammar school for the boys of Canterbury with a few additional boarders, but in the 19th century it was transformed into a public school of national standing. This was primarily the achievement of the Rev. John Mitchinson, appointed head master in 1859 at the young age of 25, a brilliant man who later became a bishop. Mitchinson was for King's the equivalent of Arnold at Rugby and Thring at Uppingham. He greatly modernised the school, introduced science to the curriculum, built the houses around the Mint Yard and tripled the number of pupils. Like other Victorian headmasters, he was a stern disciplinarian, but, in 1873, his methods seem to have provoked a revolt. Mitchinson was in the process of caning the ring leaders, in batches of seven each day, when, fortunately for the rest of the rebels, he was appointed Bishop of Barbados and abandoned his revenge.

The School's fame has not been achieved without some cost to its links with the city. One of Head Master Shirley's greatest moments, the visit to the School of George VI in 1946, showed how far King's had lost touch with local people. During the war King's had been evacuated to a safe place in Cornwall, while children in the city had borne the brunt of the air raids, spending endless hours in trenches and shelters. On 11 July 1046 King George VI and Queen Elizabeth presented the School with its Royal Charter, but nothing was done to extent their visit beyond the Precincts.

Given the long traditions of King's it is natural that the school has many unusual customs. All boys still wear wing collars. King's Scholars, as members of the Cathedral Foundation, wear black gowns during morning school, and, when assembled for Sunday Mattins, bow to the Dean and Archdeacon. School Monitors wear purple gowns during morning school and at all formal occasions. Other traditions include giving red roses to all the pupils after breakfast on Speech Day, to be worn until after speeches, when they are placed on the School War Memorial. On this occasion leavers wear 'Court Dress'.

King's has kept its traditions, while progressively making all the changes common to schools of its kind. In the arts King's became outstanding, especially by the institution of 'King's Week', a week in July when, as other schools break up for the summer holidays, King's puts on a public festival of drama and music, including a serenade in the cloisters and open-air productions of Shakespeare. The school has expanded beyond the Precincts to establish the Arts Centre (in the old Blackfriars Refectory), the centre for Craft Design and Technology (opened in 1986), and the fine new Recreation Centre, which was opened by the Old King's Scholar cricketer David Gower (born 1957) in 1990. King's is now rebuilding its links with the city and the brand-new sports facilities are to be available for city clubs. It has also become fully co-educational, and now has over seven hundred pupils.

The District of Canterbury

Whitstable, seven miles from Canterbury, world famous for its oysters, is a delightful town of charm and character. It comprises Whitstable itself and the adjacent settlements of Seasalter, a former haunt of smugglers, and Tankerton, with a castle, built 1792, now a community centre. The parish church, parts of which are 13th century, has a fine tower and was used as a look-out point for the defence of Dover Castle. Somerset Maugham lived here as a boy with his Uncle Henry, vicar of All Saints, and recaptured the years in his novels, *Mrs Craddock* (1902), *Of Human Bondage* (1915) and *Cakes and Ale* (1930), in which Whitstable and Canterbury are called Blackstable and Tercanbury.Whitstable Harbour, opened in 1832, was the first British harbour to be served by a railway and until 1952 was linked to Canterbury by the world's first steam passenger railway. The first steamboat to sail from England to Australia (the *William IV*) left Whitstable in 1835. Whitstable today has excellent facilities for water sports, especially yachting, water skiing and wind-surfing, and is a venue for national and international water skiing championships. The fishermen's cottages, alleyways and boatyards are vivid reminders of Whitstable's seafaring past.

Herne Bay was a purpose-built Victorian resort and seaside town. Its long history of smuggling is particularly associated with the Ship Inn. The first pier was built in 1832 and rebuilt at the turn of the century, but was largely destroyed by storms in 1978. The present Pier Pavilion Leisure Centre opened in 1976 and is notable for its extensive use of stainless steel. The 80-foot clock tower was built in 1837, the year of Queen Victoria's accession, and the King's Hall, opened in 1913, is one of the district's best-known entertainment venues. The nearby village of Herne is much older, with a windmill, ancient church and timbered cottages.

Along the coast, **Reculver** was a Roman fort, built in the early part of the 3rd century to defend the sea passage of the Wantsum Channel. The site of an early Christian church (*c.* 669) lies within the walls of the Roman fort (two of the original stone columns are preserved in the eastern crypt of Canterbury Cathedral). As a result of the inroads of the sea only the two 12th-century towers – the 'Two Sisters' – survive (**64**). The whole site is scheduled as an ancient monument and the towers have served for centuries as a landmark for ships at sea.

The villages in the beautiful countryside around Canterbury are well worth discovering. Listed here are just some of the most attractive within close range of the city, ideal places for a pub lunch outing. Barham, which has a copper-spired 15th-century church, was home to Lord Kitchener, who lived at

64 *The Reculver Towers were originally nearly one mile inland and are now perched on the cliff tops*

65 *Elizabethan cottages at Chilham*

Broome Park. Bekesbourne is the site of a Tudor palace and nearby Howlett's Zoo has a notable collection of tigers and gorillas. Bishopsbourne was home to the 16th-century philosopher Richard Hooker, and to the writer of seafaring novels, Joseph Conrad. **Chilham**, with beautiful timbered houses (**65**) and a 15th-century church, epitomises Tudor England. The 17th-century castle was designed by Inigo Jones and the 300-acre park is often open for falconry and jousting. **Fordwich** (**66**), once an inland port, with its own mayor since 1292 and the smallest town hall in England (the upright timbers were repaired in 1474), sits on the banks of the Stour. Five cottages overlooking the church-

66 *England's smallest town hall at Fordwich*

yard were part of a monastery, and in the most Norman church is the tomb where, reputedly, Augustine was laid in the 12th century. Littlebourne and

Wickhambreaux are delightfully situated by the Little Stour, with attractive cottages and mills. Midway between Canterbury and Whitstable part of the ancient forest of Blean, known as Clowes Wood, can be explored by a 2¼ mile forest walk, established by the Forestry Commission. The walk follows part of the track of the old Canterbury and Whitstable Railway.

Within a 20-mile radius of Canterbury there are endless possibilities to visit the coast, castles, steam railways, vineyards, and other places of interest. Broadstairs is a picturesque seaside reside where a Dickens festival is held every year. Sandwich, the northernmost of the historic Cinque Ports, is a charming old town with half-timbered houses, medieval gateways and churches; nearby are three championship golf courses. Deal is an unspoilt seaside town; boats are winched up the pebbly shore and there are three castles built by Henry VIII. Dover, famous for its white cliffs and hill-top castle, is the busiest passenger port in Britain; the Roman painted house is well preserved. Folkestone offers fine views across the Channel from the leas, a steep, cobbled old High Street and a picturesque harbour. Nearby at Cheriton is the Channel Tunnel Terminal. Hythe, a pleasant and still uncommercialised country town, offers the Royal Military Canal, the terminus of the Romney, Hythe and Dymchurch (steam) Railway, and, nearby, Port Lympne Zoo. Tenterden is one of the most delightful towns in the Weald of Kent and home to the Kent and East Sussex Steam Railway. Faversham, perhaps the prettiest town in Kent, with streets of Georgian and Tudor houses, is a centre of the hop brewing industry and sailing barges still work the creek.